Changing Chaos To Structure

How to Organize Your Life,

Unlock Secret Tools of Time Management,

and Manifest Your Goals Every Time

By **Jennifer Kates**

Dedication

To my husband Chris Kates and my son Jeremiah Kates.

Thank you for all your love and support.

Table of Contents

About the Author

Jennifer Kates is an author, speaker, certified life strategy coach, and time management expert. She holds an MBA and a Project Management Professional Certification. Jennifer Kates has accumulated many years of experience in project management where planning and staying organized are keys to success.

She has also spent over ten years speaking and mentoring young women using the experience she has gained from balancing her life as a working professional, a devout Christian, a happy wife, and a proud mother.

Jennifer loves God and loves people. She loves to organize and has a passion for helping people to organize their lives and achieve their dreams. Jennifer is dedicated to providing others with the tools and knowledge they need to lead fulfilling lives. This is why she has combined all her professional skills, her experience working with women, and her love for personal development in this book.

To find out more about the services she provides and enhance your learning, please contact her on her website, organizethreesixty.com.

Introduction

It's time to discover what your purpose is and remove the roadblocks in your way. It's time to achieve your goals and balance the craziness in your life. I'll help to give you the blueprints to birth your dreams into reality. Then, I will give you the tools, tips, and tricks to stay on track and change the chaos to structure.

> *"Do something today that your future self will thank you for."*
>
> -Sean Patrick Flanery

Changing Chaos to Structure is essential for:

- Those who want to know what their life purpose is and make it happen.
- Those who have a vision but need a strategy to birth it.
- Those who need organizational or time management skills in their life.
- Overwhelmed moms, aspiring entrepreneurs, dreamers, and busy professionals who seek work/life balance.

How This Book Is Organized

Part 1 – Master the Inner You – Before you can truly succeed at anything in life, first you must deal with your inner critic. You're the only one who can stop you from moving forward. I'll show you the proper way to view yourself, how to overcome fear, and heal from the past so you can break through any potential roadblocks standing in your way.

Part 2 – Develop Your Vision – Having a vision for your life is critical. This is the key to your success. Some people know what theirs is, and some people have difficulty clarifying their own mission. I'll show you how to discover this and make sure you aren't limiting yourself. Everything else is here to make sure your vision comes to pass.

Part 3 – Develop Your Blueprint – I'll show you how to create the bridge from where you are to where you need to be. I'll give you the strategy and the roadmap to accomplishing your dreams. I'll tell you how to plan, manage your time, create your schedule, and how to use your time effectively. You'll learn how to implement your goals and make sure your blueprint isn't overwhelming but is realistic enough to allow for the curveballs of life.

Part 4 – Let's Get Organized – Then, we'll talk about my favorite word: organization. While time management deals with productivity and the blueprint, organization helps you stay on track and helps you win every time. I'll talk about how to organize all areas of your life, how to organize your space, and how to use organizational tools to stay consistent, helping turn the chaos into structure.

Like businesses, they can have a great blueprint, but if they don't have processes and systems in place, their companies will blow up in their faces. When the business fails after the slightest curveball, like the game Jenga, the pieces will come tumbling down, and the business will be left with nothing..

Part 5 – Stay Consistent – Next, I'll tell you how to handle all kinds of distractions and how to handle different seasons of your life so you can stay on track. You'll learn how to overcome procrastination, recharge, and how to handle current obstacles you must get out of your way. We'll also talk about important rules you must not forget so you can finish what you started, knowing upfront the price you have to pay for your goals.

Part 6 – Balancing It All Together – Lastly, we'll talk about how to balance every area of your life. You want to thrive in all areas, whether it's habits you need to create or more goals you didn't think about. I'll give you tips and guidelines so you thrive and balance it all.

Icons Used in This Book

 Documents – This icon is for any documents you need to have or create to help you succeed on this journey.

 Tips – This icon is for tips to help you improve in an area of your life.

 Tools – This icon is a tool you need to implement to see results happen in your life.

Your Life Is About to Change

You have another story out there, more than you could ever imagine—a story of living your dreams. If you aren't currently happy, you don't have to stay there. It all starts with what you believe. You need your faith ignited again.

 Faith in yourself, faith in God, faith in knowing that whatever happens, you'll find a way; you'll become everything you're destined to be. It's time to write another story and be a new you. You can be the caterpillar that turns into a butterfly. You don't have to be held back anymore; it's never too late.

So, my friend, let us take the journey to transformation. No more being stuck, only thriving. I'm so excited to be a part of your journey of life transformation! Are you ready to take this journey with me? Please keep me updated on your progress by reaching me at organizethreesixty.com. Enjoy!

PART 1

Master the Inner You

Whatever your mind can conceive and believe, it will achieve."

Napoleon Hill

In Part 1...

If you want to see results in your life, you must learn to battle your inner critic. This is the first step before anything else in this book can work for you. If you don't overcome yourself, it will be like reading this book wearing broken eyeglasses: you won't be able to see right, nor should you expect to see results in your life. You'll be the one holding back.

Fix what's on the inside of you to watch change unfold on the outside. It's important to set the foundation and become unstuck. You want to be a person who finishes what you start. You can be your own worst enemy or your biggest advocate, it's all up to you.

In Part 1, I will identify three common roadblocks of the mind that can stop you dead in your tracks. These roadblocks are the way you see yourself, your fears, and the pain you carry inside, whether that's from your past or your present. All three roadblocks can keep you stuck.

My goal is to give you the steps to combat these roadblocks and Master the Inner You, once and for all.

CHAPTER 1

Your Inner World

In This Chapter, I Will:

➢ **Discuss how to see yourself the right way**

➢ **Determine different fears that might be holding you back**

➢ **Help you prevent the damage that can come from holding on to painful or negative past experiences**

Right now, you can be handed the keys to everything you need to succeed in this life, but if you don't understand how to overcome your number one enemy, those keys can be taken away from you in an instant, keeping your dreams locked up. It's like going to war without knowing who the enemy is and having no strategy: you set yourself up for failure from the beginning. If you feel you've been trying to move forward but nothing is working, it can be beneficial to take a deep look into your inner world. Often, our number one enemy can be the person staring back at you in the mirror.

The Person in The Mirror

What do you see when you peer at your reflection? How you view yourself, the words you tell yourself, and what you believe to be true will always have a major impact on your life. It will determine if you reach your destination and the shape you'll be in when you get there because your internal state will eventually mirror your life on the outside.

 As a man thinketh so is he... Proverbs 23:7

The problem is people aren't always fully aware of the power of their mind. We allow experiences and what people have told us to define who we are. When you don't understand that your mind is a powerful tool that must be mastered to find success, you'll always hold yourself back. Those who have achieved great things in life are fully aware of that. All throughout the Bible, you'll read how Jesus talks about the mind and the importance of faith.

This is a powerful lesson that changed the trajectory of my life. I grew up with a very negative mindset—I was my own worst critic. At the time, I didn't even realize how much that impacted my life. Even though I received compliments all the time, I hated the way I looked. I was laughed at a lot because I didn't know things that were common sense as a teenager. I believed I was ugly and dumb, and had zero confidence in myself.

One day, I overheard something my mom was listening to when I was in the other room. This sentence caught my attention. I heard, "You learn by the books you read and the people you meet." That's when I decided to read as much as I could, so I could learn, which was when I noticed there was a similarity of concepts with people who had succeeded. They kept talking about the power of the mind. People like Napoleon Hill, Jack Canfield, Brian Tracey, Oprah Winfrey, and the list goes on. If you pay attention and listen closely to successful people, you'll often hear similar concepts, that it starts in the mind.

That's when I knew there was something to this, and it was the beginning of my journey. Amazon and most bookstores are filled with books on the mind. Some good books I have read and ones that have been referred to me, on the mind, are below:

✓ *The Power of the Subconscious Mind* – by Joseph Murphy
✓ *The Battlefield of the Mind* – by Joyce Meyers
✓ *The Magic of Thinking Big* – by David Schwartz
✓ *Think and Grow Rich* – by Napoleon Hill
✓ *Thinking Fast and Slow* – by Daniel Kahneman

Dealing with Fear

Sometimes you can believe the best about yourself, but there's a fear you face that can't be ignored. This can be one of our biggest roadblocks, and if we let it, may cause a ripple effect like a traffic jam, clogging everything up and slowing it down. Fear is something many can relate to. It's inevitable; it's part of the process and without it, how will we learn and grow? Anytime I wanted to do great things in my life, I was met with fear.

"Everything you ever wanted is on the other side of fear."

-George Addair

When I studied for my master's degree, I was so intimidated. I was sitting in a room with other students, including a vice president from a bank, a nurse, a sheriff, and a council member, and at the time, I worked in payroll. The teacher even intimidated me. I would shrink down in my chair and try to disappear when they circled the room, asking questions. I felt like I was going to fail.

Even writing this book, the closer I got the more that fear tried to stop me. I didn't think I could actually do it. This can happen when you start something new; it's part of the journey. It's stepping out of your comfort zone—that's where the change takes place. You become a better version of yourself because you decided to get uncomfortable.

"Eighty percent of success is showing up."

-Woody Allen

Keep Putting One Foot in Front of The Other...

I also encountered a lot of fear when pursuing my dream job. I wanted to become a project manager. It was something I knew I could be good at. After I earned my bachelor's degree, I worked in a call center. I decided to leave what was comfortable and step out to get experience as a project manager by becoming a project coordinator. At the time, I didn't know that I would face an obstacle. Shortly after starting the new job, I became really sick on the job, and as a result, they let me go. My plans seemed to have fallen apart. I remember crying hard in the bathroom when I got the bad news. The experience tried to paralyze me because I took a leap of faith and failed. I no longer believed that I had what it took, so I just took any job. The new job was something I was very unhappy with.

I remember a year later, having a discussion with my husband. I told him that what I really wanted to do was project management in the engineering world, but I told him it was too difficult, and I would just choose something else I could settle with. I remember him telling me, "Jennifer, I know you can do more than what you think. I know it's in you."

7

I decided I wouldn't let the fear of my past experience hold me back anymore; this wouldn't be the end of my story, and I wouldn't give up. I kept putting one foot in front of the other. I wouldn't stop knocking on doors. Yes, some were slammed in my face. Yes, I was told, "Good luck with that," or "It will take a long time to get where you want." But I didn't stop. I gave it my best each and every time and broke through that fear. I cultivated my mind into believing in myself and not giving up.

"When one door closes another door opens; but we often look so long and so regretfully upon the closed door that we do not see the one which has opened for us."

-Alexander Graham Bell

I did thorough research to find out what skills and experience I needed and began working on that. I surrounded myself with people in that career. I worked on improving my resume, practicing for interviews, learning to sell myself, and I earned a higher education, getting a master's degree in business. I didn't give up, and I put the work into it, and the result was having my dream job and increasing my pay one hundred and sixty-three percent in a matter of three years.

I reached my dream by the time I turned thirty years old, because I refused to let fear stop me.

> *"It's the extra you did, that you didn't have to do, that got you where you are now."*

I have learned that you must have a strong mind and tell yourself you have everything it takes. Never let rejection stop you. The opportunities that were meant for only you'll reveal themselves soon enough. Never give up, and never give in.

As humans, we are comfortable with what's familiar to us, so if we aren't used to something, we don't feel safe. We don't enjoy being taken out of our comfort zone, and therefore, fear creeps in and grows. It can be difficult to push through at times, but it's crucial to get past these fears.

Give yourself the permission to feel uncomfortable. Tell yourself it's okay to feel scared; just be prepared to fight that inner critic. Do these things, and you can and will master this roadblock.

Two common fears we deal with are the fear of failure and fear of success. Let's discuss what these fears mean and where they come from, so we can stop them from blocking you in your path.

1. The Fear of Failure

A common fear that many people face is the fear of failure. You know you're suffering from this when you do the following:

- ✓ You don't finish what you start.
- ✓ You listen to the negative words in your mind and let them control how you go about your daily life, so you're constantly feeling depressed or insecure.
- ✓ You don't believe in yourself.
- ✓ You question yourself for small reasons.
- ✓ A trigger happens, and you're easily anxious.
- ✓ If someone encourages you, you don't listen.

> *"Obstacles are put in your path to see if what you want is really worth fighting for."*

Where Does Fear of Failure Come From?

1. **This can come from bad experiences that have happened in the past.** We try, and the experience fails us. We don't want to experience the emotion that came with that time again, so it's hard for us to try, believe, and act on it.

   When I was young, I had what you call, *"puppy love."* I was really close to this guy for almost two years. He was my best friend, and I felt I was in love with him. Somewhere along the line, out of nowhere, he disappeared. He dropped me with no closure, no warning, nothing.

Unknowingly, I was afraid of becoming close to another guy. After that experience, every relationship I was in, I would run from the guy if I grew too close to him. If I felt my heart was falling for him, I would bounce. I would cut them loose and not look back.

In order for my Mr. Right to not be cut from my life, I had to break through that barrier of fear. I needed to learn to love, and at the same time, guard my heart. Even if I risked losing him, even if the relationship had a possibility of failing, I would break through that fear to live my life and take every opportunity presented to me.

2. **This can come from the lies you've been fed.** Sometimes the fear arises because you have the wrong support system or are currently in a toxic environment. You've been fed lies your entire life. You've been told you don't have what it takes, or you can't do it. You've allowed those words and experiences to take control over your life, not knowing you held the power the entire time. There are many stories of people who failed over and over again, but they didn't give up. Instead, they succeeded.

Famous Failures

Let's look at some famous people who have failed, only to later succeed:

- ✓ **Michael Jordan** is one the world's most famous basketball players. Guess how many times he missed the game-winning shot? He was quoted, "I missed more than nine thousand shots in my career and lost almost three hundred games. Twenty-six times, I was trusted to take the game-winning shot and missed." Talk about pressure!

- ✓ **Tyra Banks** is a beautiful supermodel with her own show, "America's Next Top Model." On the show, she shared that she was rejected by six agencies at the beginning of her modeling career. She had plenty of people tell her no before she made it to where she is.

- ✓ **Oprah Winfrey** is one of the richest women in the world. Before she got there, she was also rejected many times. According to Become Your 1 Fan, Winfrey was fired from her evening news reporter gig with Baltimore's WJZ-TV because she became too emotionally invested in her stories. A Baltimore TV producer reportedly told her she was "unfit for television news." Thank God, she didn't let those lies stop her, and instead, she became one of the best-paid females in the entertainment industry, according to *Forbes Magazine*.

- ✓ **Walt Disney** was rejected before he birthed his dreams of Disney World. He was fired from a Missouri newspaper for "not being creative enough." The bankers rejected his dreams over three hundred times before one said yes! Walt Disney didn't give up there.

In 2018, Walt Disney World was the most visited vacation resort in the world with an average annual attendance of more than fifty-eight million people. He became a billionaire. Thank God he kept moving forward!

✓ **Many more famous people** – I could go on and on with more stories from Thomas Edison, Steve Jobs, the Beatles, Stephen King, Babe Ruth, Albert Einstein, and more. They all have failure stories, but they didn't let them stand in the way of their dreams!

2. The Fear of Success

Another fear is the fear of success. It may sound uncommon, but it happens with many people. Do you know what you carry, that you're powerful beyond measure, but you're afraid to let your light shine? Are you afraid of the power you hold? You want to take a jump, but you're scared to succeed. When you let your light shine through, you encourage others to do the same.

> *"Our deepest fear isn't that we are inadequate; Our deepest fear is that we are powerful beyond measure. It's our light not our darkness that most frightens us. We ask ourselves, who am I to be brilliant, gorgeous, talented, and fabulous? Actually, who are you not to be? You are a child of God. You playing small doesn't serve the world."*

-Marianna Williamson

Hints That You Have This Fear

- ✓ You make yourself so busy, you can avoid taking any opportunity that comes your way.
- ✓ You don't think you're worthy enough.
- ✓ You may not like being the center of attention.
- ✓ It could also simply be because of a bad experience that caused embarrassment or some kind of negative emotion.

I tried running from my gift...

For a long time, I was scared of my potential, of this powerful person I knew I had become through God. I knew that when I prayed, the heavens would open up, that I could move mountains, but I was so afraid of that power. When I was in church and someone wanted me to pray for them, I would run the other way. I ran from my calling because I was scared. I didn't realize the world needed me, that they were waiting on me, that when I allowed myself to be the best me and overcome this fear, it would have a domino effect of helping others. I was grateful in knowing that it would give people aspiration to shine and that I was giving back to God, telling Him thank you.

You must embrace your gift. You must realize that you play an important part, just like each part of our body needs each other. What if the heart were to say to the lungs, "I'm too scared to play my part. I know that I will succeed at what I'm called to do, but I'm afraid." Not only would the lungs suffer, but every other part of the body would, too.

3. The Overthinker and The Perfectionist

Overthinkers and perfectionists have the characteristics of fear. They drive themselves crazy by always thinking about the worst-case scenario. A perfectionist doesn't believe in mistakes—they can set themselves up for heartache. You can be one or both. A lot of the time, they come in pairs.

 Analysis Paralysis

The impact of having these characteristics is you end up frozen in time; you can't move forward, and the result is analysis paralysis. This is when you analyze something and want it to be perfect so much, it literally paralyzes you from moving forward. If you continue suffering from this and don't do something about it, you'll never accomplish your dreams. You'll become the person sitting behind the door, dreaming but never actually doing.

How do you know you have this fear?

The Overthinker

✓ You're constantly worried.

✓ You're easily stressed and suffer with insomnia.

✓ Your mind keeps racing and sometimes this causes internal conflict.

The Perfectionist

✓ You beat yourself up when you make small mistakes.

✓ You can't accept that human beings often get things wrong,

My good friend Gabby tends to be an overthinker. I knew she had a gift in interior design and could see her light up when she talked about it. I encouraged her to start school in it. So, we put an action plan together. As she got closer to executing her plan, she thought of everything that could go wrong. She was getting anxiety and was falling into the trap of analysis paralysis. I kept encouraging her and walking through each step. She decided to press through, and she's halfway done with school and couldn't be happier.

Strive for Excellence and Not Perfection

I used to be a perfectionist. In school, if I reached one hundred percent, I wondered why I didn't get a one hundred and five percent score. Nothing was good enough. It came from my upbringing, where there was a lot to be expected from me.

My mother grew up in a third-world country in the Philippines. She slept in one room with eight siblings and her parents. She would sometimes sleep on the table as she dreamed of a better life. Her dream came true when my father brought her to America. She wanted to make sure I didn't go through those same struggles, so she always pushed me to be the best I can be.

I was always hard on myself and would beat myself up every time I made one tiny wrong move. It wasn't until one of my high school teachers came to me and told me an expression I'll never forget. She said, *"Jennifer, strive for excellence, not perfection."* I soaked in those words and gave myself room to learn and grow.

Bad Experiences You Hold Onto...

Maybe you believe the best in yourself, and you've overcome fear, but getting to that finish line is hard because of all the baggage you carry. Sometimes it can be extremely difficult to even think about your dreams with the cards you've been dealt in life. Many of us have experienced real pain and trauma, and that can be hard to shake.

How do you get rid of the poison from the past? How do you move forward when something has died inside you, when you've built a wall so thick to protect yourself from being hurt again? Maybe painful words tell you that you would never be anything and that you're worthless. What if you're currently living in that nightmare, feeling like you're in quicksand and barely breathing? You know it's like a cancer growing inside you, but you don't know how to let go and get your power back. I'll tell you in the next chapter what helped me overcome traumatic events in my life.

It's Time for Change

It's time to master your inner critic, remove the roadblocks of fear, and release the bad experiences you've held onto. Refuse to be a person who stands in front of the door but never walks through it, who never fulfills their potential. Refuse to be a person who dreams but never has the courage to reach for them.

No, you deserve to experience life's best right now. No more being held back. You want to become unstoppable. It's time to tear down the dam that has been holding up your blessings.

It's time to realize the power you hold so you won't forget for a second that nobody but yourself can stop you. It's time to experience purpose, happiness, joy, freedom, and more.

Lessons

Three common roadblocks to your success:

1. How you view yourself
2. The fears you deal with
3. The negative experiences you hold onto

How you view yourself

o If you feel like you've been trying to move forward but nothing is working, it's very important to take a deep look into your inner world. Often, our number one enemy can be our own reflection.

o How you view yourself, the words you tell yourself, and what you believe to be true is going to play a major impact on your life. It will determine if you reach your destination and the shape you'll be in when you get there because what goes on inside you'll eventually mirror your life on the outside.

o Those who have achieved great things in life are fully aware of the power of their own mind and have learned to control it, to be rid of any negative thoughts or energy.

Dealing with fear

- You must realize that on the other side of your fear is your dreams.
- Two fears you can come across are:
  o Fear of Failure

       o Fear of Success

   • Characteristics of Fear:

       o The Overthinker

       o The Perfectionist

       o Both can result in analysis paralysis

Bad experiences you hold onto

       o To get the best in life, you must free yourself from the mental prison.

       o You have to release the very thing taking your power and holding you back.

       o If you don't, it's like a cancer growing inside you.

       o You can't drive your car by constantly looking in the rear-view mirror.

CHAPTER 2

Overcoming Your Roadblocks

In This Chapter, I Will:

> ➤ **Guide you as you face the truth about your roadblocks**
>
> ➤ **Provide you with tools to get to the root of what's holding you back**
>
> ➤ **Help you change your perception about yourself, fear, and your negative past experiences**
>
> ➤ **Teach you to become a problem solver**

Imagine running the track, and at the finish line, there's another part of you, cheering you on and telling you to keep going and not give up. It's the future you, the best version of yourself. There are so many great things for you. But as you strive to finish the race, you hear all of these people on the sidelines, screaming in your ear that you can't do it. You turn your head towards them, and fear causes your heart to pound inside your chest. You slow your pace and wonder if you really can do it. Don't allow yourself to be defeated. Reaching your goal often becomes the hardest right when you're about to finish. This is your most important test.

Let's talk about ways to overcome roadblocks in your life.

Step 1. Acknowledge the Source

The first step is to acknowledge the source. Most of us have heard the expression, "A drug addict can't be set free from being a drug addict unless he knows he's one."

You can't go to a different place if you don't even know where you are. Just like with any other obstacle, you must first be honest with yourself. You can't fake the funk. Many of us put a band aid on something traumatic before going into the denial phase.

Those in Denial

- ✓ You put on a mask and tell yourself nothing happened.
- ✓ You understand what has happened, but you've disassociated yourself from feeling the experience. You put it on pause and keep yourself busy.
- ✓ You act like everything is okay and push the experience under the rug.

All three examples only work in the short term, but do not heal the wound. If you suppress it, it's like a woman stopping the birth of her baby from coming out. When women are pregnant, they have to feel those contractions to push the baby out, or they have to feel the pain of getting an epidural. One way or another, they have to get the baby out. One way or another, there will be some pain and fear.

Acceptance

The way to your freedom and your healing is by being honest with yourself. Part of acknowledging it comes from accepting it. It can take humility and vulnerability to do this. That's why you can't ignore a virus in your body or act like you aren't sick. You can't put it on pause or tuck it away. No, to fully heal, you have to eradicate that thing.

Embracing Fear

When I was a teenager, I spoke in front of hundreds of inner-city kids. I was thrown onto the stage, and I was paralyzed with fear. I was very introverted at the time. It was way out of my comfort zone to be speaking on stage. I would have never known at the time that this would develop into a gift, into something I was good at. It didn't happen overnight. The more I spoke in front of people, the better I became.

> *"You don't have to be great to start, but you have to start to be great."*
>
> -Zig Ziglar

I went from being paralyzed and looking down the entire time I was speaking to looking at one person in the face. The next thing I knew, I was walking all over the stage in my zone. It doesn't mean that fear went away. I've spoken many times to many people, I still get nervous, but it dissipates as I start. You have to be courageous in it.

"Courage isn't the absence of fear; it is acting in spite of."

-Mark Twain

Accepting the Pain

You can't just say, "I don't want the pain," "I don't want the contractions," or "I don't want the epidural." You'll continue to be stuck. You don't want to abort the process. Sometimes you must go through the ugly parts of life to uncover the good. Processing what you went through helps the fear become much easier to control.

Acknowledging the source of your problem doesn't make you weak; it makes you strong for being brave enough to face it. Sometimes it's painful to be honest with yourself but necessary for your freedom. Once you've acknowledged the source, you can move on to step two.

My good friend Tina had finally saved up enough money to buy her own house and completely paid it off. A year later, she received a horrible phone call from a neighbor that her house was on fire. She rushed home paralyzed as she watched her house burn down. The next day, she acted like nothing happened. She had nightmares but kept pushing it off.

Later on, when she tried to move forward in life, she realized something was wrong. She couldn't feel emotion. I talked to her about the importance of going back to that place and accepting what happened so she can heal from it. Tina did just that, and she finally cried. She never let the tears go, and she allowed the healing process to take place. It freed her.

 # Step 2. Get to the Root

Acknowledging that something is wrong is the first step, which is to dig deeper and find where the seed is and uproot it. To get to the root, ask yourself some tough questions. Use the why format. Every time you come up with the answer, ask yourself why. The point is to keep challenging your thoughts.

I'm close with my Aunt Miranda who ran a small daycare out of her own home. She's married and has beautiful grandchildren. Aunt Miranda felt like something was missing in her life. There were things she wanted to do to improve her life. She wanted to work on her dental health, overcome her fear of driving, become a better version of herself, and open up a bigger business. When she thought about pursuing these goals, she was immediately faced with fear. She told herself, "What am I thinking? I can't do any of these things." Let's see how Aunt Miranda can dig deeper into why she thinks she isn't capable of improving her life.

Example of the Why Format

- *Question 1: Why are you afraid to improve your life?*
- *Answer: What's the point? I'm not worth it.*
- *Question 2: Why do you think you aren't worth it?*
- *Answer: Because I failed in the past.*
- *Question 3: Why did you fail last time?*
- *Answer: Because I'm a failure.*
- *Question 4: Why do you think you're a failure?*
- *Answer: Because my father told me I was a failure. I'm scared to drive because my father told me I was a hazard to myself and everyone on the street. My dad always told me I was worthless, a quitter, a failure, and so I always believed I couldn't do it.*

Do you see how Aunt Miranda kept digging into why she felt the way she did, and she got to the root? She was afraid to improve in any area of her life because she believed the words her father told her, that she was a failure. The root of her fear started with her father. This is the story she grew up telling herself. Aunt Miranda's life will soon change when her story begins to change. What story have you told yourself?

Help from a Trusted Person

Sometimes it's hard to figure it out ourselves. We can disconnect our mind from how we feel. Sometimes it takes talking to a trusted friend, a therapist, or an expert in the field to help you gather your thoughts and get to the root of things. I suggest a trusted friend, someone who can point you to God, someone who has experienced what you experienced and survived. Not a person who is a negative naysayer, who is known to gossip, and poisons your mindset with more fear. Also remember, God is the ultimate source; He normally speaks to your intuition.

Be cautious when listening to advice from people. Some people tell you from looking out of their own lens, their own experience, their own pain, and their own insecurities, but that doesn't mean it has to be your story. Take things with a grain of salt, use wisdom, be prayerful about who you talk to. You don't want people to control your life and make decisions for you. It's very important to know the difference.

Get the full view. Get out of your head and talk with someone you trust. Aunt Miranda decides to go to talk to someone she trusts about her thoughts. She talks about the pain she has experienced growing up with all the negativity in her upbringing. The person she confides in helps her to find the root of her fear.

Step 3. Change Your Story

Anytime you want to change something in your life, you must start with the mind. The story you've been telling yourself, the story you've attached to your life must change. You can't rehearse the same story that's keeping you stuck. It doesn't work that way. Change your world; change your mind. Please don't just skim over this step; go back and chew on it until it sinks in. It doesn't mean that you act like nothing ever happened. You find the lesson and use that as fuel to grow and be stronger. Do this in faith.

Insanity is doing the same thing over and over again and expecting different results.

-Albert Einstein

Negative Thinking

No more toxic thinking about yourself. Receiving and believing negative thoughts about yourself is like a poison that can spread in your life. Negative words can brainwash you into believing lies. People will tell you that you can't do it. They'll say, "good luck on that." They'll mock you, laugh at you, and think they are better than you. Pay attention to the words you receive from others and the words you tell yourself. Sometimes we become immune to how negatively we have been thinking. I keep reiterating these same concepts because it's a major obstacle anytime we want to undertake something great in our lives.

Remove Toxic Thinking

Step 1. Replace negative thoughts with positive thoughts: Negative thinking won't take you to the next level. You must do something different to get a different result, and that means creating a new way of thinking.

When Aunt Miranda discovered the root of her fear was the lie her father told her, she changed her story. Instead of rehearsing and nursing all the negative words her father said, she told herself that her father was broken and miserable; therefore, he tried to project that on her life. She realized; I'm somebody amazing. I have made mistakes, but I learn from them, and I excel at whatever I do. She fell in love with who she was. She scheduled someone to teach her how to drive. This resulted in going places she always wanted go. She worked on her dental health and felt so good. She made plans to start her own business, and she thrived. Her life was completely changing for the better. That fear no longer held her back. That new script she's telling herself is so powerful. To make it leaps and bounds in this world, you can't skip this process.

Two Ways of Thinking

❖ **Remember who you are.** *In Jeremiah 1, God says, He knew you before He formed you in the womb. Psalms 139:14 says you're fearfully and wonderfully made in His image.* To bring yourself down, to question who you are and what you're capable of, means you're questioning the Creator of the universe. Don't forget your original design. If you knew you came from a king, wouldn't you act differently? The ways in which other people have defined you, your mistakes, your experiences do not define you. Only God can define you.

During one of my darkest days, as I vented to a friend, he checked me. I was acting weak minded and wanted to give up. He said, "Who lied to you and told you that? You have enough power inside you to change so many things." He reminded me of who I was, someone I had forgotten.

Have you forgotten who you are? Do you even realize how powerful and amazing you are? You must know you have everything it takes! Don't forget who you are and whose you are.

My friend's words echoed in my mind when he asked me, "Who lied to you and told you that you couldn't do that?"

I had to dig deep within myself and ask where did those bad beliefs come from? Why did I believe that I was so weak? What happened to the strong Jennifer? What happened along the way?

❖ **You must believe the BEST of yourself.** Once you remember that you come from the King of Kings, the next step is to believe the best of yourself. You need to see yourself as a new you—the *best* version of you. Anytime you start a new endeavor, be prepared for obstacles to test you. You must have a belief in yourself so strong that no one can break it. You must believe you're capable of this, then get the proper tools, have the road map laid out, and trust the process as you move forward, tackling one milestone after the other. Don't let anyone tell you that you can't do anything. When I said I was going to marry my Mr. Right after college, I was told, "Don't get your hopes up." But I was determined to be that person and trust God, and my desires came true. Find affirmations to tell yourself and hold fast to what you believe!

Step 2. Keep retraining your mind until it becomes second nature

Anyone who has mastered a skill has practiced it over and over again. I used to be my own worst enemy and had to retrain my mind so I can pull myself out. I had to learn to believe the best in me.

When my life was dark, and I felt like I was falling off a building, about to crash any moment and lose everything I worked so hard for, I had to remember how to fight and beat this. I had to tell myself over and over that I could beat this. When my heart was breaking into pieces from the hurt people caused me, I told myself I would never love again, and I would be this bitter single woman. I had to tell myself, "God has the ability to heal my heart." I told myself that over and over again until it was in the fiber of my being. I had to change the narrative.

Once you've gone through these steps and framed a new way of thinking, you've now mastered the person looking back in the mirror. You become a force to be reckoned with! Now, let's tackle how you view fear.

Change the Definition of How You View Fear

If you have the right perspective, you see failure in a positive light. Change the definition of how you see failure; this is very important. Two people can see failure in different ways. There are many positive words for this. For some, it's learning, growth, and self-improvement.

In a professional setting, we can call it a "discrepancy," which means a variance, that something is off. Failure can simply mean feedback. The data provided can be used to help you improve.

Thomas Edison

Thomas Edison invented the light bulb, but it didn't come without failure. He made a thousand mistakes, but chose to see them as lessons. He saw failure in a positive light.

"I have not failed. I've just found 10,000 ways that won't work."

-Thomas Edison

Step 4. Be a Problem Solver

Now that you understand the importance of how you view yourself and how to get rid of the toxic thinking, you understand what fears you're dealing with and how to view fear in the right light. It's time to take practical steps to remove these roadblocks once and for all.

Step 1. List the Problems and Possible Solutions – Grab a piece of paper and do a brain dump of everything that concerns you. This means to get everything on your mind written down. It doesn't have to be organized; you just dump it on there like you would throw puzzle pieces on the floor. Once you do that, look at each concern and write down possible solutions to your problem.

For example, Jerry can't stand his job. He needs an exit strategy. He needs to create a plan to leave his job. Some people just walk out, but they are worse off because they didn't come up with a plan. They can't pay their bills or find a job for months.

Anytime I have left my job, I come up with a plan that leads me to success. That means knowing where I want to go next, finding out what didn't work at my current job, so I don't make the same mistake again. I know what questions to ask in interviews. For example, maybe I didn't like the mandatory overtime at my job, so when I interview for the next jobs, I know to ask if overtime is mandatory. If it is, I know not to accept that job.

An exit strategy means updating my resume, touching base with references, and creating a document of all the places I will apply to. This document will show the website, the company name, the job description, the pay, the date I applied, and any other pertinent information. That way, if someone reaches out to me, I know what it's for or if I want to follow up. Do you see how this exit strategy is much better than just walking out the door with no plan?

Jerry doesn't need to complain and do nothing about it because it doesn't do anything to help the problem. He makes a list of problems and writes down a possible solution and plan to his solution.

- Problem: I can't stand my job.
- Possible Solution: Find another job
- Plan: Exit Strategy
  - Find out what it's I want
  - Find out what it will take to get there
  - Gain the skill or experience needed
  - Update my resume
  - Job hunt
  - Prepare for interviews
  - Voila – Strike! He's at the job he loves, instead of just sitting there complaining and do nothing about it.

Step 2. List Best-Case and Worst-Case Scenario – On that same list, write down the best-case and worst-case scenario for each problem. You can think of the best thing that can happen if you proceed with the decision, and you can think of a realistic worst-case scenario that can happen.

Jerry decided to go more in depth about leaving his job, so he creates a best-case and worst-case scenario list, if he goes with the solution of planning an exit strategy for finding another job.

Jerry's List

- *Best-Case Scenario: I find a job quickly, and I absolutely love it.*
- *Worst-Case Scenario: I think I can find a better job, only for it to be worse off than the other.*

He can have more on his list, and then he weighs the pros and cons. Which list is longer, the pros or cons? Can he do anything about the worst-case scenario? Yes, that's when he creates three plans.

Step 3 Create a Plan – A lot of people just talk about what's going on and wonder why they are so stressed out. Write out the things that are bothering you. You can't visualize being the best speaker and not practice or be clear on what you want to talk about. You need to be solution oriented. Here are three plans to help you solve your problems.

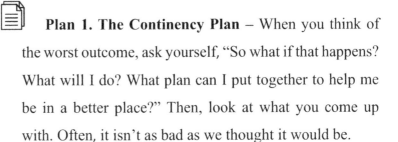 **Plan 1. The Continency Plan** – When you think of the worst outcome, ask yourself, "So what if that happens? What will I do? What plan can I put together to help me be in a better place?" Then, look at what you come up with. Often, it isn't as bad as we thought it would be.

Jerry decides to create a contingency plan. A contingency plan is in place if the worst-case scenario happens. That means for Jerry, he ends up at a job worse off than the one he was in before. His contingency plan could be to have another exit strategy until he finds the best path forward. This makes him feel a little better so he knows he isn't stuck and can still proceed with his plan.

Plan 2. The Preventative Plan – Another plan to create is a preventative one. When you know of a possible issue that can happen, you can work on preventing it from happening to the best of your ability. This takes some brainstorming.

In Jerry's case, his plan is to do thorough research on the company. He also researches key questions to ask in the interview to see if this is something he likes.

He asks about business culture, management style, mandatory overtime, and the duties of the job, and this helps him gauge if it's something he wants to do. This plan is much better than not having one at all and wishing and hoping for the best. Remember, where there's a will, there's a way.

Plan 3. Plan B – This is another solution to your problem. If the first one doesn't seem to be working, it may be best to have a backup, which is something you can do to evaluate and weigh the pros and cons.

Let's say Jerry has analyzed his choices, and the pros and cons of finding another job wouldn't be in his best interest right now. Maybe Jerry just has a problem with his job duties and management. So, a Plan B is for him to apply for another position in the company with a role he enjoys and new management. This could resolve his problem. The point is, if you seek out solutions, you can resolve your fears.

Lessons

Four steps to finding the leak

1. Acknowledge the source
2. Get to the root
3. Change your story
4. Be a problem solver

Step 1. Acknowledge the source

- You must be honest with yourself.
- You can't get rid of what you don't know is there.
- Being in denial only works in the short term, but the way through your freedom and healing is being honest with yourself.
- Part of acknowledging is accepting it.

Step 2. Get to the root

- To remove anything in your life, you have to find where the seed is and uproot it.
- To get to the root, ask yourself tough questions. Use the why format.
- If you can't do it yourself, ask a trust friend, therapist, or expert in the field.

Step 3. Change your story

- o Remove toxic thinking
  - ➤ Step 1 – Replace negative thoughts with positive thoughts.
    - Two ways of thinking:
      - o Remember who you are
      - o Always believe the best in yourself
  - ➤ Step 2 – Keep retraining your mind until it becomes second nature.
- o Change the definition of how you view fear
  - ➤ Ways to view failure
    - Learning
    - Growing
    - Self-improvement
    - Discrepancy

Step 4. Be a problem solver

- o Step 1 – List the Problems and Possible Solutions
- o Step 2 – List Best-Case and Worst-Case Scenario
- o Step 3 – Create a Plan
  - ➤ Three Plans
    - The Contingency Plan
    - The Preventative Plan
    - Plan B

CHAPTER 3

Healing from Your Pain

In This Chapter, I Will:
- ➢ **Discuss how holding onto pain can hinder you**
- ➢ **Give steps on how to heal properly from pain**

Sometimes it takes more than acknowledging, getting to the root, changing your story, and coming up with plans to solve your problem. Sometimes it takes true healing from the past. The door to your dreams is thin, and your baggage won't fit through the gap. These wounds can be painful to revisit, especially if the experience was a traumatic one. Letting go doesn't always happen overnight. It's a process. Sometimes experiences come that stab us so deeply, it's hard to sleep, breathe, eat, think positively, or even be the same person you once were. There are tools to your healing process.

A broken heart...

I used to be the person who couldn't heal from the pain of the past. Growing up without a father to guide me, I was naïve and therefore, subject to people who took advantage of me. These experiences tried to tear me down to my inner core.

When I found out I was cheated on in different relationships growing up, it tried to make my heart black and break me. It was a constant stab in my heart. It brought anger, anxiety, and depression in my life. I began a pattern of thinking. My script was "*I always get cheated on,*" and guess what, that's exactly what happened.

I decided it was time to change my reality, that I would no longer accept this story in my life. I rewrote my script by saying, "*This pattern breaks today; no longer does this happen to me.*" I attract faithful, good men and have true friends. Guess what? I began to attract the right men in my life and hence, I married one.

This can be a difficult process and easier said than done. Your mind is a battlefield, and the enemy is constantly trying to break you. My mind was always at war, but I had to keep reminding myself of my new way of thinking until it was second nature. I had to fight through it. If you aren't careful, you can do this wrong. Let's look at ways to do it right.

Step 1. Watch Out for the Victim Mentality.

As you find out where the pain comes from, pay attention to your thought process. Be careful that you don't fall into the trap of a victim mentality. Your situation was real, and it isn't something to be dismissed. The problem is many people stay trapped and give their power away when they have a victim mentality. Most times, people with victim mentalities do not see that they have fallen into this trap.

A Victim Mentality

- ✓ You play the blame game. You're always pointing the finger at the other person/experience and never looking inward on what you could do differently.
- ✓ You nurse and rehearse the past over and over again.
- ✓ You show no responsibility that you have the power to respond.

I had every right to be bitter. I was betrayed over and over again. I had a right to be angry. But as I continued to hold on to the anger, the pain, and the bad memories, I realized it did nothing but strip happiness from my life. It became this weight that would always hold me back. I had to make a hard decision that only came from deep within. I had to make the decision that these experiences would no longer define me. I couldn't be miserable and say you're the reason why I'm this way, why I no longer trust anyone. If I did that, I gave that person my power. I couldn't act like nothing happened when I knew my heart was hard. I knew that being honest with myself, that was the way to my breakthrough. I had to be humble enough to know it was my choice to choose to have a victim mentality or not. When I stopped playing victim, I got my power back.

Step 2. Find the Lesson from Your Experience.

It's important to see what could have been done differently and what you can take from this experience that will cause you to be to become better and not bitter. Finding your lesson means you become a better version of you from that experience.

It isn't always easy to find the lesson when you were the one who was done wrong. For me, I discovered how strong I was, that there was purpose in my pain, and that in my testimony, I could help people find the steps to inner healing.

 # Step 3. Forgiveness.

You have to dig deep within yourself and make a conscious decision to let go of the baggage. This is part of the healing. To do this, find your why. Then, you need to forgive yourself, then the other person. This is part of getting your power back.

Sometimes in the past, I have said I have forgiven someone, but when you see that person or think about that issue and it changes your mood and your attitude, then you haven't forgiven them. This has happened to me a few times.

It takes mental blocks, going deep in your mind and letting it go, accepting they were imperfect, and giving it to God. Remember God forgave you in your mess. You didn't deserve His forgiveness, you were imperfect, but God forgave you.

It doesn't mean you dismiss what happened, but it means you release all those negative emotions, letting go of that anger, hurt, and

43

pain. You use wisdom going forward. You forgive them, you forgive yourself, and let that healing energy flow. You let God turn your mess into a message.

All things work together for good to those who love God, to those who are called according to his purpose.

-Romans 8:28

🔧 Step 4. Allow the Healing Process to Take Place

Understand that you're human, and sometimes there's a grieving process. It will take the power of God to help you get through this. It's okay to feel this way, just don't stay stuck there. Trust that the healing process is working. Once you have your wound cleaned and stitched up, believe you've done the right thing. Let time work its course.

Trust in the Lord with all your heart and lean not on your own understanding; in all your ways acknowledge him, and he shall direct your paths.

-Proverbs 3:5-6

I remember after I had a C-section with my son, the next day I tried to move. The doctors were surprised. I still was very sore and couldn't even lie down on a bed. I had to lie on the couch and take pain medicine. My body was healing, and it would take time. As long as I didn't do anything to reverse the process, I would be fine.

So many people go back into what hurt them in the first place. Sometimes that's just a different face, a different experience. They don't allow themselves time to properly heal. Some of us think something is wrong with us because we are still hurting. Wounds take time to heal; keep investing in yourself, renew your mind daily, and surround yourself with positivity. Create a new version of you.

Remember you'll find love from within yourself, and that comes from God, not others. What many people fail to realize is the love that they are searching for, the healing they are searching for, they can find it in other people. You soon realize people fall short of your expectations. The love and healing you're looking for comes from the God inside you.

God will fulfill that hole you've been looking for in others. He will help you heal, and what can take people several years to get over, He can do in an instant. He can give you a new heart. That's what God did for me. I gave Him my hurting, broken heart, and in exchange, He gave me a new, healed one.

Step 5. Use Your Situation as a Testimony to Help Others

Learn to let the past go, so it no longer has power over you. Channel that negative energy into positive energy to become a better you. Help others, use your situation as a testimony, and turn your mess into a message. Do not let the past paralyze you a second longer.

Even though the bad experiences come from the enemy, it didn't take God by surprise. He's turning your situation around. You'll overcome. Someone out there's going through what you went through. They need to hear your story; they need to know how you made it.

 # Step 6. Be Grateful and You'll Attract More of That into Your Life

Remember to take care of yourself. Enjoy the present moment. Celebrate the good things in life. Too many times, I hear people complaining when they have much to be grateful for. It bothers me because I know that person will remain stuck until they become someone who can focus on the good things.

Be the person who looks at the glass half full, not half empty. Write down everything you're grateful for and focus on that; you'll soon attract more of that into your life. Remember someone out there has it was worse than you, and they are grateful for what they have.

> "When life gives you a hundred reasons to
> cry, show life that you have a thousand
> reasons to smile."

 # Step 7. See It in Your Mind

Picture in your mind yourself healed, succeeding. Picture the best you. You have to see it in your mind before it can happen. Visualize the best outcome—the future you want. Think best-case scenario and focus on that. This is a powerful technique that works when you believe it. If you have to speak in front of a large audience, don't see yourself messing up and others laughing at you; see yourself doing excellent, and the people being engaged.

Visualization Techniques

When I was going through the hardest times in my life, I kept seeing myself drowning, trapped, falling off a building, in a car about to crash. It wasn't until I told myself that I had already seen the end of this chapter and I had made it, I began to see myself succeeding. Instead of drowning, I saw myself standing up in the water. Instead of being trapped, I saw myself with a sword, tearing through the cobwebs. Instead of seeing myself falling off a building, I saw myself with wings. I was flying and cutting every strong hold that tried to bring me down. I was no longer in the car about to crash.

See it in your mind, and you'll soon see it in your life. You can now take practical steps to mastering the inner you.

Lessons

Seven steps to healing from your pain

1. Watch out for the victim mentality.
2. Find the lesson from your experience.
3. Forgiveness.
4. Allow the healing process to take place.
5. Use your situation as a testimony to help others.
6. Be grateful, and you'll attract more of that into your life.
7. See it in your mind.

Step 1. Watch out for the victim mentality

o The problem is many people stay trapped and give their power away when they become a victim.

Step 2. Find the lesson from your experience

o Finding your lesson means you become a better version of yourself.

Step 3. Forgiveness

o You're getting your power back by forgiving.

o When you see that person or think about the issue and it changes your mood, your attitude, you haven't forgiven them.

o Remember God forgave you in your mess.

Step 4. Allow the healing process to take place

- o Sometimes there's a grieving process.

- o It takes the power of God to help you get through this.

- o Trust that the healing process is working.

- o Remember you'll find love from within yourself, and that comes from God, not others.

Step 5. Use your situation as a testimony to help others

- o Turn your mess into a message.

- o Someone out there's going through what you went through.

- o They need to hear your story; they need to know how you made it.

Step 6. Be grateful, and you'll attract more happiness into your life

- o Be the person who looks at the glass as half full, not empty.

- o Write down everything you're grateful for and focus on that; you'll soon attract more of that into your life.

Step 7. See it in your mind

- o You have to see it in your mind before it can happen.

PART 2

◁◆▷

Develop
Your
Vision

Then the Lord answered me and said: "Write the vision and make it plain on tablets, that he may run who reads it. For the vision is yet for an appointed time; but at the end it will speak, and it will not lie. Through it tarries, wait for it; because it will surely come, It will not tarry."
Habakkuk 2:2-3

In Part 2...

After you have Mastered the Inner You, you can now see clearly and start with the right mindset. The next part to living your best life is to have a vision. You can't skip this part. This is the next building block of the entire puzzle.

This vision is what drives you and gives you the key information you need. Your vision starts with the desire that God put in your heart. If you can see it in your mind, you can birth it into your life. Playing out the vision in your life brings pure joy. Your vision is powerful, and it will be what you hold onto when the storms of life try to wipe you out.

In Part 2, I help you discover the vision for your life by discovering who you are. Then, I will teach you how to harness the power of your vision. You'll learn the importance of vision boards, how to create them, and the rules to manifesting your goals into your reality.

CHAPTER 4

Discover Your Vision for Your Life

In This Chapter, You Will:
- ➤ **Learn to understand who you are**
- ➤ **Learn to understand your season**
- ➤ **Learn to create vision statements for your life**

E veryone is on a different path in life. Some people know exactly what they were born to do. They may have a ten-year plan mapped out, while others have no clue what their vision is. They go with the flow, not knowing where they'll end up. Many people fall into the middle. Then, there are those who follow someone else's vision, not their heart's desire.

It's important to discover what your mission is, so you don't fall into the traps of the system. You don't want to become someone who is complacent and just exists when God wants you to fulfill your purpose.

Where there's no vision, the people perish.

-Proverbs 29:18

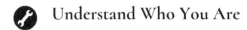 ## Understand Who You Are

Most people start off by not knowing what their vision is. Don't feel alone. Life is all about discovering who you are and what your purpose is and then making it happen. When you discover who you are and the way God wired you, your vision becomes clearer. This is when you can craft vision statements to take you to the next level. It doesn't always happen overnight. It's a journey. The first step you take on the journey is learning more about yourself.

Question Guide to Self-Discovery

Ask yourself questions and seek out the answers to find out more about yourself.

- What are you naturally good at?
- What are your strengths and weaknesses?
- What do you really like? What makes you smile?
- What does your closest family and friends say you're good at?
- What are some things you would like said about you at your funeral?
- What legacy would you like to pass down?
- If you had only so much time to live, what would you want to do that you haven't done?
- Where do you see yourself in five to ten years from now?

Personality Tests

Another way to find out more about yourself is to take personality tests. The types that I really like are Myers Briggs, Disc, OSPP, and the Enneagram. There are plenty more out there. You can also use aptitude tests. Even your birthday, what your name means, your environment—they all play a part.

A Guide, Not A Box

The Bible says we are fearfully and wonderfully made in His image. He created us. So, don't let personality tests box you in. There are some weaknesses that have become your strengths. Use them as a guideline to help develop yourself into a better you. Once you have a clearer understanding of who you are, focus on your strengths and match that up with your passion, and that will help you narrow down what you want to do.

The Myers Briggs

The Myers Briggs is by far my favorite. If you haven't taken the test, I highly recommend it. My former manager even used it at work. Churches have brought it up. My teacher in high school introduced the tests to me. It really opened my eyes. I was so shocked on how on point it was. I had a lot of my close family and friends take it, and they felt the same.

Information to Take Each One

1. The Myers Briggs Personality
   - https://www.123test.com/jung-personality-test/
   - Then, go to the Jung personality test.
2. DISC
   - https://www.123test.com/jung-personality-test/
   - Then, go to Disc personality test.
3. OSPP
   - https://openpsychometrics.org/tests/O4TS/
4. Enneagram
   - https://www.truity.com/test/enneagram-personality-test
5. Other Resources
   - Books:
     - ✓ *"Strengths Finder,"* by Tom Rath
     - ✓ *"Wired That Way"* by Marita Littauer & Florence Littauer
     - ✓ *"Discover your God-Given Gifts"* by Don Fortune
     - ✓ *"The five love Languages,"* by Gary Chapman

Create High-Level Vision Statements

After you've done some soul searching and researching, write down some vision statements for your life. Start off high-level. Think of the bigger picture, of the vision of what you want your ideal life to look like. Once you create this, we'll break them down into goals.

"Whatever your mind can conceive and believe, it will achieve."

-Napoleon Hill

Examples of Vision Statements

- I want to be the best version of myself in every area of my life: spiritually, mentally, emotionally, financially, relationally, physically, and intellectually.
- I want to fulfill my God-given purpose by…
- I want to be financially independent by doing…
- I want to enjoy time with my loved ones and travel around the world.

Understand Different Types of People

Sometimes you may know yourself, but you still don't necessarily know what you want. Everybody is wired a certain way; we all have different backgrounds, different personalities, and different experiences.. You bring a strength that others don't.

Let's discuss three types of people:

1. The Spontaneous Type

There's the spontaneous type of personality. They are free-spirited. They are the type of people who go with the flow. They don't really want to write about their future. They prefer to take things one day at a time. For these personality types, I encourage you to still have a vision and a goal, so you don't just end up anywhere.

2. The Confused Type

The next person is the "confused" type. The confused type can fall into one of the categories below.

- ✓ I'm at a fork in the road, and I don't know which way to go.
- ✓ I keep changing what I want, so I'm not always quite sure what I want.
- ✓ I have too many voices in my head. I'm not sure what I really what.

✓ I have an idea of what I want, but I have no clue how to get there.

3. The Organized Type

Lastly, there are the people who know exactly what they want. They are organized and have five to ten year goals planned out in each category. These tools and techniques will excite you. If you fall into this category, look for the gaps in this book. See what you're missing and implement it into your life.

I've been in all these categories, and the three steps below helped me gain more clarity.

🔧 **Step 1. Understand which voice you're listening to** – The first step is to understand which voice you're listening to. Sometimes you're confused because you have different voices from close family, friends, or significant others who have told you this is your future, but it hasn't resonated with you. You need to ask yourself who put this vision in your heart. Is this your authentic self?

🔧 **Step 2. List the Pros & Cons** – The next step is to list pros and cons on what you're confused about. Sometimes you can't make sense of things because you don't have enough information. This is when you need to do some problem solving. Weigh the pros and cons on paper. Do your homework. As you begin to work out the positives and negatives, things will become clearer. Then, you can take the calculated risk.

Step 3. Seek God – Other times, it may be that you don't have peace, and you can't quite put your finger on it. There may be a reason why you're not at ease. Sometimes your intuition is speaking to you. If you don't have peace, stay still, pray, and wait until you have your peace, then take a leap in faith. God said seek and you'll find. Not just pray, hope, and wish it'll come. Everything will become clearer as you take one step at a time as God guides you.

Ask, and it shall be given to you; seek, and you'll find; knock, and it will be opened to you.

-Matthew 7:7

Understand Different Seasons

There are also different seasons that come into your life that can impact the route of getting to your vision, which doesn't have to change on a global level, but only sublevels. It's like going through a maze and depending on what season you're in, will determine what path you must take to reach your destination. The different seasons in your life can be relationships, responsibilities, and obstacles. For relationships, you can be in a season where you're single, dating, married, have children, or a combination of them.

1. The Single Life

In your single life, it's really important to lay the foundation down. You'll still have a lot of responsibilities. You want to be a whole person for yourself and if you meet your significant other. It's important to invest in who you are. Investing in yourself means accomplishing goals for your life, following your passion, educating yourself, learning to love yourself more, and becoming a better version of you.

A lot of times as you're walking in your vision, your significant other is right there, as a whole person as well. You attract that into your life, as likeminded people attract likeminded people. You grow leaps and bounds when you can master your single life.

2. The Dating Life

When you're dating, you want to make sure that person shares the same vision as you. You can ask questions to find these things out. You don't want to end up sacrificing your dreams because the other person isn't in agreement with your vision. You don't want to end up butting heads so much that it jeopardizes your relationship.

When my husband and I started dating, I remember shutting the door and being frustrated. I told myself, I can't do school and date. I'm either so focused on him that school goes out the door, or I'm too focused on school, and I don't have time for him. Luckily, we shared the same vision, and he came to complement me, not take away from me. He helped me through my studying and reaching my vision.

3. The Married Life

When you're married, every problem you had in your single life will just magnify. It's important that both of you know your vision. You can't mix two visions when yours isn't fully defined. Two people who don't know where they're going end up in the wrong place. That's why it's vital to be on the same page before you're married.

Also, you'll want to think how you'll both do things together. Who's doing the chores? How do you both manage your finances? What are your weaknesses and strengths? What do you all value, and where do you both butt heads? Is there a lack of love and respect? How are you investing in your marriage? In chapter fourteen, I'll show you how to balance everything to strengthen your marriage. Your vision will be a combination of both of yours because you're one.

3. Parenthood

Throwing kids into the mix, all I'm saying is you better have your stuff together, or you're in for a rude awakening, as everything just amplifies. You'll have a new normal, and it will most likely change every year as kids come with different challenges at different ages.

I think it got easier for me when my son was around four; by this time, he was more independent, and the diapers were gone.

Some parents feel overwhelmed, like they can't do it. You could be doing it all by yourself with little or no help. You may be barely functioning off sleep. It can be a tough season, but be encouraged; you can still be successful. There are thousands of parents who have found their niche, some worse off than you. It's possible, you just have to be more strategic on what you do.

There's this beautiful girl I mentored growing up named Heather. I call her my little sister. She went to college, but life had thrown her some curve balls. She ended up pregnant twice, and the fathers were nowhere to be seen. To make things even harder, she would meet other guys that would end up tearing her down. She stopped going to school, and life became extremely hard raising two little girls, as a young adult, with little to no help.

She was frustrated because she had all these dreams, and she felt like it went out the window. She didn't think she could make time to go to college again and do the things she loved like health and fitness. She was just working and working to take care of her girls. She was depressed and broken.

Heather is a fighter. She knows there's something great inside her. Through the depths of darkness and with a lot of fight and God's help, she picked herself back up again and dared to dream big. She has gone back to college and is almost done with her nursing training. She's focused again on health and fitness. It does require work when doing it with two girls by herself, but she's doing it. She's pushing through it. She knows the investment is worth it, and she wants better for her girls. Heather refuses to let the hardship of parenthood and her past hold her back.

Understand Different Responsibilities

Another season that can take you on a different path is the type of responsibilities you're dealing with. Your responsibilities can change. This is why everyone's situation is so different and why it's important to understand where you fall. A thousand things can be thrown into the mix. You can use the concepts in this book to create a strategy for your success.

Different Responsibilities
- ✓ A teenager in high school.
- ✓ A young adult going to college.
- ✓ A working professional.
- ✓ A single mom working long hours.
- ✓ A full-time mom with a full-time business.

Large Obstacles

Another large season that can take us on a different path are the types of obstacles we face. So many of these can be thrown at us from losing a loved one, dealing with a sickness, divorces, depression, and an endless series of things. Life can knock us down where we feel like we can't breathe. Sometimes when we're in the storm, we're just trying to survive. It can be hard to dream. I've been there.

Trust is everything to me, and when it's broken by someone you gave your heart to, it can leave you depressed and lost. My worst fear is being betrayed by someone I love. When this eventually happened, I was devastated. My world changed at that moment. It's really hard to focus on goals when you're broken, angry, and lost. The motivation just isn't there. There were times I didn't want to sleep, eat, or even move from my bed. It took a lot to pull myself up and dream again, hope again, and believe again. I knew if I stayed there, I would just get run over by life. I had to pick myself up. One thing that helped me during this time was my anchor—God.

Key – Have an Anchor

One key tool to help you in the difficult seasons is to have an anchor. Storms will come to try to knock you off your feet. That's why it's important to have an anchor to help you through. You have to focus on the good things. You have to take one step at a time, find what helps you, and find someone to talk to. It's okay to go through it but just know how to bounce back. Don't stay too long because if you just sit there and do nothing, you'll end up drown.

Anchors can be your relationship with God, close loved ones, a statement you hold onto, a promise you made to yourself. Some anchors can be kids, a person's legacy, or a person's purpose.

Make Your Vision Clear

Okay, so now that you have more of an understanding of what personality you may fall under and what season you may be in, you can take this into account when you're working towards creating your vision. The next step is to make your vision clear. This is the next building block into helping make your dreams come true.

Lessons

Understand who you are

- o Life is about discovering who you are and your purpose and then making it happen.
- o Ask yourself questions and seek out the answers to find out more about yourself.
- o Take personality tests.
- o Create high-level vision statements.

Understand different types of people

- o The Spontaneous Type
  - ➤ These types must build a foundation.
- o The Confused Type
  - ➤ Step 1 – Understand which voice you're listening to.
  - ➤ Step 2 – List the Pros and Cons.
  - ➤ Step 3 – Seek God.
- o The Organized Type
  - ➤ Use these tools and techniques in the book.
  - ➤ Find the gaps and add to your system.

Understand different seasons

- o The Single Life
  - ➤ It's importation to lay the foundation.
  - ➤ Likeminded people attract likeminded people.
  - ➤ Invest in yourself.

- o The Married Life
  - ➢ Every problem you had in your single life will just magnify when you're married.
  - ➢ You can't mix two visions when yours isn't fully defined. Two people who don't know where they're going end up in the wrong place.
- o Parenthood
  - ➢ Everything just amplifies.
  - ➢ This can be a tough season, but you can still be successful.
  - ➢ It's possible; you just have to be more strategic on what you do.

Understand different responsibilities

Large obstacles

- o Have an Anchor

CHAPTER 5

Harness the Power of Vision

In This Chapter, I Hope You Will:

➢ **Learn about the paradigm shift**

➢ **Discover why vision boards are powerful**

➢ **Understand how to create a vision board**

➢ **Understand the rules to manifesting your vision**

When you understand the power of your subconscious mind and harness its power, everything will change for you. Your subconscious mind is different from the conscious mind. Your conscious mind is what happens when you make decisions. It's what you're aware of in the present moment.

Your subconscious mind is what happens when you aren't even focusing in on it. It tells your body when to breathe, blink your eyes, and digest your food. It's working even when you're asleep. It holds memories you can't even recall. It's often how we're programmed. The subconscious mind influences the conscious mind on what to do, while the conscious mind makes the decision.

The subconscious mind is very powerful, and whatever you feed it, you become. What you think about the most, you most likely will attract in your life. This is the Law of Attraction.

Understanding and applying the power of my mind was a game changer in my life. When I learned how to reprogram my entire thinking through my subconscious mind, I attracted better things into my life.

You are a living magnet. What you attract into your life is in harmony with your most dominant thoughts.

-Brian Tracy

The Paradigm Shift

Because of your upbringing, you were programmed in a certain way, and it can be a challenge to change your way of thinking. That's why in the Bible, Romans 12:2b says, *"to be transformed by the renewing of your mind."* When you change the way you perceive things, you create a paradigm shift within yourself. This is where the change begins.

The paradigm shift is how you reprogram your subconscious mind. Part of reprogramming your mind is to look at visuals. Visuals are the language of the subconscious mind. A vision board can help with those visuals and give you focus.

The Power of Vision Boards

A vision board is powerful, lifechanging, and it works! A vision board is a visual representation of your dreams, goals, and what brings happiness to you, put on a board. Not only does it transform you, but it also brings you focus and brings things into your life.

Steve Harvey said, "I would be in trouble if I didn't have a vision board." He understands how powerful vision and vision boards are. He's saying if he didn't have it, he would be worse off than where he is. It made a huge impact in his life.

Oprah says, "Vision boards absolutely work; you need plan to execute so that every step moves you into that vision."

Jim Carey used a form of visuals. In 1985, he wrote himself a ten-million check for acting services rendered. He dated it ten years into the future and kept it in his wallet. Guess what? He made ten million exactly ten years later! There are so many more examples, just take a look on the internet.

When I've done vision board workshops, I've heard many stories of people who started a vision board and used the strategies I taught them, and they saw big things happening in their lives. My nephew acquired his own trucking business, my friend got promoted into a management position, and another friend found her Mr. Right. They all came back and said, "Wow, this really works."

Why I Chose to Use Vision Boards

I was introduced to vision boards at nineteen years old, in the toughest part of my life. I had just ended a relationship and needed a new focus. I was a depressed teenager because I didn't have my father, my mother and I fought all the time, and I experienced betrayal from friends and relationships I was in.

At the time, I wasn't thinking about goals. I was more focused on all my problems. When I made my first vision board, I decided what the heck, let's dream. I knew my mom couldn't afford to put me through college the entire four years. So, I thought about getting scholarships and graduating from college. I found a picture of me in my high school graduation outfit, and I placed it in front of the college I wanted to graduate from. I put scholarships around that image.

I decided to expand my dreams and put on my vision board that I would be a businesswoman, making great money, marrying a good guy, having a child, living in a beautiful home, and being a strong woman of God. I even dared to dream on having my own business. At the time, it was farfetched, but a girl could dream, right?

The vision boards helped me to focus on the goals I put on them and to believe I could actually do it. It shifted my focus from my problems to my future. As I put the action towards achieving these goals, I was shocked that everything on my vision board came true, little by little. So, I made more vision boards throughout my adult years.

The scholarships unexpectedly came. Not only did I graduate from college, but I ended up being the face of the school. They put me on their magazines, websites, brochures, commercials, and flyers. I even went to get my master's degree in business. Who would know the naïve girl who didn't know much could actually do this?

Even the vision of marrying a good guy happened. On my vision board, I had a picture of the type of husband I wanted with words all around it. One day, this guy from church helped me move. He walked past my vision board, stopped, turned around, walked up to it, and read the section about my husband. He said to himself, "Wow, that's exactly me, I wonder what it would take her to notice." Fast forward to many years later, he's my husband and the father of my son, and I thank God daily for him! The dream job, the husband, the house, the book, the business, they all came one by one.

It wasn't easy; I was tested by faith, trials, and it takes work. But the vision board was a catalyst to get me on the right track. I admit there were times I wanted to give up. I even threw a vision board away, but I started again.

God Gets All the Glory

Make no mistake about it, God gets all the glory. I couldn't have done this without Him. Follow His laws, do your best, and God will do the rest. He will open doors that no man can shut. You'll know it's from Him when it's rooted in love, not selfishness, or a goal you want to accomplish because you're trying to compare yourself to others.

How to Get Started

 ## Step 1. Find Out What You Want

For those who know exactly what they want, it will be easier to find things for your vision board. If you aren't sure what you want or fall under the category of a spontaneous person, understand that it's okay. A lot of people start off this way, and that's how I started.

You can do what's called opening and allowing. That means you're open to dreaming. You allow whatever it is that makes you happy and puts a smile on your face, and put it onto your vision board. You see a kitten, and that makes you happy? Add that on there. Pull from your vision statement that you've created.

 ## Step 2. Gather Your Supplies

There are those who are in different seasons. You can have what are called themed vision boards. Maybe you're about to have a baby, have fitness goals, are about to get married, or want to go on a vacation. You can have a vision board just for that. Now, let's get the supplies. Depending on what type of vision board you do will depend on what supplies you have.

Different Styles of Vision Boards

✓ **1. Traditional Vision Boards** – A traditional vision board is one with a poster and pictures from a magazine cut out. For this, you'll need scissors, glue stick, magazines, and a board. You can get magazines for less than a dollar at the thrift stores. You can also go to hair salons, ask people, etc. I would also recommend grabbing images or pictures you want to include and get some markers.

✓ **2. Digital Vision Board** – A digital vision board is one that's displayed on any technical device. This can be your computer, tablet, or phone. This is my favorite one. This is good for those who are tech savvy because sometimes it can take a long time if you don't have the right magazines.

For example, I have a digital vision board of my dream home. I found a luxury home I really loved and put it in my PowerPoint. I didn't stop there. In each PowerPoint, I put pictures for each room. My son had a playroom, I created a gym room, a game room, and more. The backyard had a beautiful pool that I made sure to screenshot and add to my digital vision board. By the time I was done, I had every detail of how I wanted my dream home to look like.

Tips for Putting Together a Digital Vision Board

 Tip 1 – Use Microsoft Office Products – For the computer, you can use one of the Microsoft Office products like PowerPoint, Visio, or Word. Then, go to Google, type the word you're looking for, and copy and paste it into one of the apps. For example, if you want abs, go to Google, type abs, then click images, scroll down until you find the right one you want, copy, and paste it into whichever type you're looking for.

 Tip 2 – Use Your Screen Saver – To make it even more fun, you can snip a picture of your face and add it onto the body. Then, play how you want it on the document. You can then keep it there to look at or print it out and use those images to combine to the traditional vision board. Another thing you can do is use your phone through a collage. Screenshot, cut out from the website, and make a collage. Then, add it as your screen saver or however you want. This can be done quickly.

 Tip 3 – Cork Boards – A cork board vision board is what it says in the name. For these vision boards, you just need the board itself, some thumbtacks, and the images you want to put on there.

Tip 4 – Word Vision Board – Another type of vision board is a word vision board. A word vision board just has words on the poster. These words can be quotes, Scripture, inspirational statements, anything related to your goals and encouraging yourself. You just need a poster and something to write with for these vision boards.

 Tip 5 – Journal Vision Boards – A journal vision board is a journal with your images in there. The benefit to this type is that you can take it wherever you want to go. You only need a journal, scissors, images, a glue stick (less messy), a marker, and voila! You can even create a scrapbook.

 ## Step 3. Collect Images and Words

Once you have your tools, you can search for the images and collect them. an envelope if you think you'll run out of time and are going the traditional route. That way, any images you cut up can go in the envelope, and you can pull it out the next time you start.

Once you've collected everything, lay it out how you want. You could have one that flows naturally without any particular structure, one poster for each category, or you could lay them out in different sections across your vision board. There's no right or wrong way to do it. It all depends on what you're looking for and the positivity you wish to see in your own life.

Laying Them Out in Categories

- ✓ Spiritual
- ✓ Finance / Career / Business
- ✓ Family / Home / Vacations
- ✓ Fitness / Health

 ## Step 4. Put the Images Together and Hang It Up

When you've done this, glue the images on there. I recommend laminating it for extra security. You don't want the images on your vision board to fall off easily or for it to easily get ruined. I have used vision boards with no lamination, and they haven't lasted long.

Laminating lasts forever, and it also makes it look more presentable. Once this is completed, place it somewhere you can look at it every day. This can be your office, the living room, your bedroom, wherever you know you'll see it. Try to review this daily.

The Rules to Manifestation

Some people have vision boards, but nothing manifests in their life. They don't understand that they're missing key ingredients. It's like trying to unlock a door using a combination lock. You must get all the numbers right.

For the chosen things to manifest in your life, you should follow these nine rules.

Rule 1. Have Unshakeable Faith

How do I know if I don't fail? How do I know if God will answer my prayers? You must have faith in the result. Read that slowly. You need to believe you're capable of it, that one way or another, you'll make it. You need to be confident with every fiber in your being. It can take time to get there but focus on getting to that point.

> *Faith is the substance of things hoped for, but the evidence of the things not yet seen.*
>
> *-Hebrews 11:1*

I remember working at a job I didn't like. Management was rough, I was being overworked and underpaid. I remember trying to have some goals on how to transition into a better job. One of them was an easy way out but didn't make that much or wasn't as satisfying. The other goal was my dream job. I would make good money, and I would be happy. I remember telling my husband that it would be too difficult to get to my dream job. I didn't have everything it took, so I'll just go the easy route and do something that I may not necessarily be happy in, but it's better than nothing. I remember he told me, *"I just know you have what it takes."* Over time, I believed that. It was that faith that helped me get to that exact dream job.

 ## Rule 2. Get in Alignment

Do not focus on what you don't want. Don't make the mistake I did for a while, which many people fall into. They think, "Oh, I have my vision board. I'm doing my declarations. I'm believing, so why isn't it happening?" They don't realize they're actually focusing on what they don't want.

You must be in alignment. This is what the Law of Attraction means. The energy you have needs to match the energy you're attracting into your life. When I wanted a husband and put him on my vision board, I declared it, but then I focused on how lonely I was and wondered when he would come. If you're focusing on what you don't have, you'll get exactly that. You need to feel you already have it because your subconscious matches the frequency of what you feel.

I played love songs and felt the emotions of happiness so I would attract that. I imagined that my Mr. Right and I sang the love songs to each other. There's power in how you're feeling while you're imagining what you want. Catch yourself if you focus on what you don't want. Then do something to change your feelings of positive emotion to match what you want.

Rule 3. Let the Vision Come from the Right Heart

The third rule is to make sure your vision comes from the right heart. The right heart means it doesn't come from vengeance, hate, or any negative emotions. The reason we want it to come from the right heart is because God's hands are on it, and He can bless you. He widens doors that no man can shut, and he closes doors no man can force open. You can tell it's from the right heart when it matches positive emotions like the Bible talks about in Galatians 5:22-23.

> *But the fruit of the spirit is love, joy, peace, patience, kindness, goodness, faithfulness, gentleness, self-control; against such things there's no law.*
>
> *-Galatians 5:22-23*

Rule 4. Pass the Test of Time

The fourth rule is to pass the test of time. I'm sorry, I wish I could tell you that it worked like a microwave, like Dorothy in the

> *To everything there's a season and a time for every purpose under heaven.*
>
> *-Ecclesiastes 3:1*

Wizard of Oz where you think it, tap your heels, and out it comes. But everything has a season, and there will be the test of time.

You have to let the seed grow and keep feeding it with the right tools. If you follow everything else I have and will teach you, it will come to pass. What you sow, you'll reap. Focus on enjoying the journey and trusting God's timing. Pass the test of time.

 Rule 5. Trust in God

Sometimes you may think you've finally attained it, only for it to be snatched out of your hands. You have to trust that one day, you'll look back and be glad it didn't happen that way, or you would have missed out on the amazing thing you have. You have to trust in God's overall plan. You must know it will all make sense soon, and something better is on the horizon.

I remember when I was eager to get my first house, I found the perfect house. I did everything to get this application through. I was so excited; it was ours, so I thought. Come to find out, someone else took it right underneath me. I was disappointed because I wanted that house.

Shortly afterwards, I ended up getting an even better house. I also found out the house I didn't get had a leak in the roof! You must trust God and know he will give what's right for you.

> *"Sometimes good things fall apart, so*
> *better things can fall into place."*
> *-Marilyn Monroe*

Rule 6. Focus on the Result

Keep in mind that we won't always know the exact steps to get there. Focus on the result, then take one puzzle piece at a time. We won't always know the how upfront; that's when God gives us piece by piece as we show more action and commitment.

Rule 7. Understand that Words Are Powerful

Speak affirmations; words are powerful. Declare, speak in the now. Don't use the future tense because then it stays in the future instead of now. You want to activate things in your life now. Get a list of declarations, and thank God that it's happening now, even if you don't see it. Let it come to pass with using one of the tools, the power of declaration.

The tongue has the power of life and death, and those who live it will eat its fruit.

-Proverbs 18:21

 Rule 8. Act

You must act. Don't think this rule can be skipped. Some things are motion activated. Ever come up to a door, and it automatically opens? What about when you put your hands underneath a faucet and the water comes out? Nothing would happen until you move.

I find time and time again that people are complaining because they don't see anything happening in their life, but they're doing nothing about it, absolutely no action. Please don't be one of these people. Having a dream but no action towards the dream is wishful thinking.

"An idea not coupled with action will never get any bigger than the brain cell it occupied."

-Arnold H. Glasow

Rule 9. Stop Complaining

For the love of God, please don't sit there and wonder why nothing's happening if you haven't done skip diddly do. If all you've done is complained, have excuses, saying you're waiting on God, maybe God is waiting on you. Maybe He's saying, "I gave you all the tools, now it's up to you to make it happen." What are you doing? Examine your thoughts, words, and actions. Change your complaining words to what you're doing and line them up with positivity.

I kept complaining about not losing weight, but I was eating what I wanted and didn't work out. When I stopped the complaining and worked on my nutrition, fitness, knowledge, and habits, my body transformed.

> *"When I lost my excuses, I found my results."*

Time to Create the Bridge

Now that you have your vision, your vision board, and you know how to harness the power of vision, it's time to break them apart and create systems and processes customized specifically for you. It's time to create the bridge from the present to the future and then do the action part so you can live your reality!

This is the part where most people become stuck, and this is why I'm here to help you, if you're ready.

Lessons

The subconscious mind is powerful; whatever you feed it, you become.

The subconscious mind is your default system. It tells your conscious mind what to do.

The conscious mind is logic; this is where you reason and make decisions.

How to design vision boards:

- o Step 1 – Find out what you want.
- o Step 2 – Gather supplies.
  - ➢ Different styles of vision boards.
    - • Traditional.
    - • Digital.
    - • Cork Board.
    - • Word.
- o Step 3 – Collect Images and Words
  - ➢ Lay Them Out in Categories
- o Step 4 – Put the images together and hang it up somewhere you can look at it regularly.

The rules to manifestation

- o Rule 1. Have Unshakeable Faith
- o Rule 2. Get in Alignment
- o Rule 3. Let the Vision Come from the Right Heart
- o Rule 4. Pass the Test of Time
- o Rule 5. Trust in God

- o   Rule 6. Focus on the End Result
- o   Rule 7. Understand Words are Powerful
- o   Rule 8. Act
- o   Rule 9. Stop Complaining

PART 3

---◁◆▷---

Develop
Your
Blueprint

" A goal without a plan is just a wish."*
-Antoine de Saint-Exupery
Saint-Exupery

In Part 3...

You can have the most amazing ideas in the world, and you can believe in yourself so strongly, but without instructions to get there and the actual execution, it's often just wishful thinking. To do the work, you need a proven strategy. This is called a blueprint, and it shows you how to get from Point A to Point Z. This is just like when builders work on a beautiful house. The designer knows that just having a vision isn't enough. They must create the actual design, with every detail intricately thought out.

In Part 3, I help you break your vision into goals and then your goals into tasks. I show you how to manage your tasks and develop a schedule customized for your life. Once you're done with this, you'll have your blueprint.

CHAPTER 6

The Power of Goals

In This Chapter, I Will Help You:
> **Learn how to break your vision into goals**
> **Write goal statements correctly**
> **Manage tasks**

It's time to put together the recipe to your vision, which is a step-by-step action plan to see your goals come to pass. It is the bridge to get from where you currently are to where you desire to be. I first discovered the importance of goals when I was young. I kept reading quotes and seeing all these successful people talk about goals. I wondered, "What's so important about these goals?"

Then, I read a book called, "Power of Focus," by Jack Canfield, Mark Victor Hansen, and Les Hewitt. The book said to write down one hundred goals. That's when I challenged myself. Some of my goals were to mentor young women, go to college, get married, have a child, get a house, get a good job, travel, publish my own book, start my own business, and become financially independent. These goals came from my overall vision. For me, those goals matched my vision of fulfilling purpose, having freedom to spend more time with my loved ones, doing the things I love, and being the best me in every area of my life.

Vision Versus Goals

A vision is an image of what you desire to be. It's the complete picture. A goal is a milestone, something you accomplish to help you reach that vision. A goal is more detailed. I'll give you some examples of writing your vision down versus goals. We'll begin at a high-level.

Example 1 – Finances

Vision Statement

My vision for my life is to be financially independent, living in a big, beautiful home, and not working for anyone but myself.

Goals

- ✓ To be debt free
- ✓ To be financially savvy
- ✓ To save X amount
- ✓ To invest X amount
- ✓ To make six figures

Example 2 – Health

Vision Statement

My vision for myself is to be at my ideal weight and to be healthy.

Goals

- ✓ To eat better
- ✓ To work out more
- ✓ To understand more about nutrition and fitness
- ✓ To food prep
- ✓ To get a trainer
- ✓ To get an accountability partner

 ## Get Crystal Clear on Your Goals

Now that you know the difference between writing your vision and your goals, it's time to break your goals into more detail. The more detailed you are, the better chance you have at achieving your goals.

To get crystal clear on your goals, you can follow the S.M.A.R.T acronym from George Doran. Many goal achievers are aware of this acronym and use it often in making their goals clearer.

I like to use the other acronym that has E.R. at the end, making the word, S.M.A.R.T.E.R. Let's discuss what each letter means and how to implement it into your goals. I'll give you an example of one of my goals, of wanting to get a house, and how I used this acronym to get more detailed.

S – Specific

Be specific with your goals. Be able to answer questions like what, when, where, why, and how. Record all of the things you want to see digitally or on paper and give yourself time to process them before you put them into action. Sometimes it takes some homework to know how to write a realistic goal. You may have to figure out your schedule first.

When I first wrote I want to buy a home, that wasn't specific enough. What time of house did I want? Where did I want to live? What type of neighborhood? A better way for me to put is I want to buy a big house in Tulsa, Oklahoma, in a nice neighborhood. I could even describe what big means and what a nice neighborhood means. Now there are more words I need to put into this statement. Let's see what's next.

M – Measurable

Your goal needs some numbers to measure it against. For me, I can add how much money I want to spend on my home.

A – Attainable

Is your goal attainable? It needs to be realistic, as you don't want to burn yourself out too quickly or lose motivation before you even begin. It's good to dream big, but make sure your timeframe is realistic, and you have all the proper tools to make it happen.

Was my goal of wanting a house attainable at the time? I know I need money and good credit to buy a house. If I didn't have either one of those, it may not have been attainable at that time, but since I know that I could work my way towards that goal, it's realistic in a certain season.

R – Relatable

Make sure your goals relate to your vision. It's okay to have a goal to buy a purse or start a hobby. That's fine, just remember to think big and make sure it's a goal that comes from what you want to do, not on what others are pressuring you to do.

If my vision was to live in an apartment my entire life, then having a house isn't relatable to what I want to do. If my mother was always pressuring me to buy a house, and that wasn't what was in my heart, then this goal isn't relatable to my vision.

T – Timebound

Set a deadline for your goals. It's okay if you have to change it up but try hard to stick by it. Setting a deadline is crucial and can make a world of difference. This is one of the keys that has helped me reach my goals. I understand that stuff comes up, and I can't always make the deadline, but putting the deadline there at least challenges me to get things done.

I tell myself I want to purchase a $150,000 big, beautiful house in a nice neighborhood in Tulsa, Oklahoma in two years. From there, I can break my goals down into tasks that I can focus on each year, month, week, and day to move towards my goal. If I didn't have a deadline, the goal just sits there on a piece of paper with no plan on moving into action.

E – Evaluate

Evaluate your goals. I recommend consistently reflecting on what's working and what isn't. You can even do this daily if you like. Each week, I pull up my Word document listed, "Monthly Goals" and journal my progress.

R – Reward Yourself

It's important to reward yourself when you've accomplished a milestone of any size. What that reward is, is up to you. Only you know what you struggle with the most, or what's the most achievable for you, so treat your accomplishments accordingly. You can celebrate with family and friends, buy yourself something you've wanted for a while, or do something special. Just take time to recognize your hard work with a reward.

Speak in The Present Tense

One important note when you finalize your goal statements is to change it regularly from the future tense to the present tense. You need to write it as if it has already happened. This is a powerful technique. You're activating your subconscious mind and the Law of Attraction as if it has already happened, instead of it staying in the future. There's power in exactly what you say.

I change the words in my sentence from, "I want," to "I have." I have a $150,000 big, beautiful home, in a nice neighborhood, in Tulsa, Oklahoma. I can still add my timeline to work towards my project of three years, but I tell myself that I have it now, to activate the Law of Attraction. I'm currently writing in the house that I once had a goal about. I will be following these same steps for the next bigger house I want. Follow these steps when getting crystal clear on your goals, and you're one step closer to achieving them.

Lessons

- You need goals; they're the bridge to get from where you currently are to where you desire to be.
- A goal is a milestone, something you accomplish to move you closer to your vision.
- Become crystal clear on your goals using the S.M.A.R.T.E.R technique.
    - o S – Specific
    - o M – Measurable
    - o A – Attainable
    - o R – Relatable
    - o T – Timebound
    - o E – Evaluate
    - o R – Reward
- Speak in the present tense

CHAPTER 7

Managing Tasks

‛‛

In This Chapter, I Will:

> ➤ **Teach you how to break goals into tasks**

> ➤ **Help you categorize and prioritize your tasks**

> ➤ **Provide you with the tools to estimate how long your tasks will take and create milestones**

‛‛

So far, we've discussed how to write your vision and how to write your goal statements. Now, it's time to break your goals into small pieces that you can focus on, called tasks. Tasks are the *"action"* parts you work on to help accomplish your goals, and these are what you implement into your schedule.

I'm always breaking my goals or projects down into tasks when I plan weddings, manage million-dollar projects, or even manage the several things going on in my life. I need these tasks to make things happen. One thing to make note of before you break your goals into tasks is to understand if your goal is something that's ongoing or a project.

Habits / Routines / Rituals

If your goal is ongoing, it may be more of a habit, routine, or ritual that you want to accomplish. A habit's something you end up doing without even thinking. A routine is something that may take more effort to process, where you may have to work on your schedule. A ritual is similar to a routine but has more meaning to the action behind it.

If you break your goals down for something ongoing, it may be more about adjusting your schedule, replacing bad habits, and creating a plan to be consistent by reviewing and tweaking until you've accomplished that. Once it becomes second nature, and you don't need triggers to remind you, then you move on to the next goal.

For example, Nancy and Logan want to create a habit of saving twenty percent of their money to put towards their house. It doesn't require a lot of brainstorming to do that. It means simply creating a plan to make sure that happens → acting → creating consistency → reviewing any tweaks → tweak if needed → consistent → Habit accomplished.

Projects

A project has a beginning and an end. For example, planning a vacation, having a wedding, getting your degree. Once you accomplish that goal, it's complete. There's nothing further for you to do.

For goals that are projects, planning will be a little more in depth, and there will be more tasks involved. Projects need to be broken down further, and it's crucial to have a project schedule.

How to Break Goals Down into Tasks

Breaking your goals down into tasks can be tricky. If this is the case, you'll need to do some homework. First, you can look for an expert, someone who already has done it, and follow their guidelines. This can save you time. If you can't find an expert, do your own research.

 ### Step 1. Research

To do this, start off with researching the overview of the subject—the bigger picture. From there, you can go down the rabbit trail. When you research the overview, you can ask specific questions, which will lead to others, and the result will help with making an educated decision. It will help you discover what you don't know. This can be a missing ingredient to the puzzle you need to complete.

For example, when I wanted to write and publish my own book, I had no clue what to do. I didn't know anyone personally who had already written a book, so I couldn't ask them. I didn't feel like paying a bunch of money to find out. Therefore, I chose to do research.

Before I got into the weeds, I just researched the overview. I learned the steps to publish my book. I went to several websites and made notes. I found out there were sections for creating a rough draft, to reviewing the book, to publishing and marketing the book. In each of those categories, I researched even more things. In reviewing my book, there are different ways to do that. I didn't know about beta readers, alpha readers, and all the different types of editors. It was my continued research that set me up for success.

I also did this in my career; I found out what it would take to become a project manager, and through my research and putting a plan together, I followed it until years later, it happened. I had to get the information, not just talk about it and think it would fall into my lap.

Step 2. Get All the Puzzle Pieces

What do you do after you have a lot of notes from your research? You organize the tasks. First, do a brain dump. This isn't difficult if you've done your homework. You just gather all the information, advice, and what you know to make your goals happen and dump in one location. One location can be a piece of a paper or a Word document on your computer.

Dumping all the information into one place can feel messy. It's just like a bunch of puzzle pieces in a box. You empty it out by throwing the puzzle pieces on the floor. Don't worry about the mess, you can clean it up later. The point is to have all the puzzle pieces so that later, you can prioritize and put it together.

Think of any research or planning you need to do. Do you need to budget? What action items do you need? What about reviewing? My brain dump was on the computer. I took my research from all the websites and just had it all on one document, not organized, just dumped in there.

Categorize Your Tasks

After you've done a brain dump to the best of your ability, you should have many puzzle pieces that are tasks. Now, you want to categorize these puzzle pieces, and there are many ways to do this. One way is to categorize the pieces into different phases. Lay out a piece of paper with a bunch of sticky notes to categorize each puzzle piece or move things around on your computer.

 ### Category 1 – The Research Phase

The first phase is the research phase. This is where you may not know what to do, and you need to get more information to create your blueprint. So, find the puzzle pieces that have anything to do with research. If you're well aware of what to do, this process may be skipped.

The next step is to go through that messy document and find out what items in there need further research. Find out what an alpha reader is? Find out what different types of editors they are? Place all those tasks under the category of research. When I write my second book, I can skip the research phase because I've already done this, and I'll just follow my guidelines I already created.

Category 2 – The Planning Phase

The second phase is the planning stage. You need time to plan and put together your action items. That's your blueprint. Find any puzzle pieces that have to do with planning. Do you need help from a third-party vendor? Do you need to plan a budget? Do you need a project schedule? Planning requires organizing tasks.

For me, I needed to plan a budget for my book. This would require more research. I need to put a schedule together for my book and find out who would be a part of my book. Who would be doing the cover, my pictures, my marketing, my website, my book trailer, and more? A lot of times, research and planning go hand in hand.

Category 3 – The Action Phase

You need time to act. This is where we have our tasks plugged into our schedule, and we act, act, and act! This is where we see things come to fruition. Any puzzle pieces that have a verb need to go under the action phase. For me, that started with writing my book each day. For this would go under that category.

Category 4 – The Review Phase

Do checks and balances to make sure you're staying on top of things. It's easy for actions to fall through the cracks, so keep yourself accountable. Any puzzle pieces when it comes to managing, reviewing, and tweaking your plan should go into the review phase.

I had an accountability partner each week who would see how I was doing with my book and staying on task with my schedule. I highly recommend having someone keep you accountable. I also would journal each week to see what was working, what was I getting behind in, and how I could tweak in. Now, you should have your puzzle pieces more organized. You can always do subcategories within those categorizes. This may be easier for the advanced.

Prioritize Your Tasks

Once you've cleaned up your pieces, you can prioritize the puzzle pieces, so you're ready to plug them into your schedule. After I was done categorizing all my tasks to publish my book, I needed to prioritize them, so I know which one to focus on first. Sometimes they can happen at the same time.

Step 1. Start Forwards or Backwards

When you prioritize your puzzle pieces, either start from what you can currently do now all the way until the goal has completed, so you're looking forward. You can also start backwards by thinking of the big picture and keep breaking it down backwards.

For example, when I wanted to become a project manager, it was easier to think backwards using the big picture. What does take to become a project manager? I need a lot of experience managing projects and even having a project management professional certification can help. What do I need to get that experience or certification? Once I have that answer, I keep breaking it down until I have everything I need. That's how you start from the big picture and go backwards.

Step 2. Ranking

Sometimes the information is so much that it can be hard to prioritize in one sitting, so the next step would be to rank them in order. You can do this based off the information you already know. I know that I can't become a project manager without experience, so I know experience is ranked first before applying for a project manager position. In the example below, I have a list that's not in a certain order yet, so I rank them to help me put them in order.

- Get my project management professional certification 3 (or 5)
- Get experience in becoming a project manager 2
- Research everything it takes in becoming a project manager 1
- Apply for a project manager position 4

Prioritizing

Now that I have ranked them, I can prioritize them in order. It's okay if some things are happening at the same time. The point is to get as close as you can in prioritizing your tasks. The example below is my new prioritized list to become a project manager.

- Research everything it takes in becoming a project manager 1
- Get experience in becoming a project manager 2
- Get my project management professional certification 3
- Apply for a project manager position 4

Time to Estimate

Once you've prioritized your list on each of the categories, it's now time to zero in on each puzzle piece to determine how long it will take to complete. This will help prepare the tasks to put into your schedule

Estimate How Long Each Task Will Take

You want to have a schedule where you see a task, you accomplish it, and repeat. That's how you see things manifest in your life; it's that easy. To do that, you need to get the tasks into your schedule. The puzzle pieces will fit under five categories when it comes to time: yearly, quarterly, monthly, weekly, and daily.

Step 1. Estimate – Your Best Guess

Before you can put these puzzle pieces in these categories, you need to have an idea of how long each puzzle piece will take. It's okay if you aren't spot on; that's why we say estimate instead of actual. Estimate means your best guess.

If you have experience, you'll be more accurate. You can research or ask experts in the field if you aren't sure. If all else fails, give a rough estimate based on what you know. Sometimes within the puzzle pieces, you need to break them down even smaller, and estimate the smaller puzzle pieces to get the estimated time of the bigger puzzle piece.

Greg and Mindy want to get married and have a beautiful wedding. They've already done their research and talked to experts. They get their puzzle pieces under the action phase and put estimates together. Let's just grab a few puzzle pieces to see how they estimate.

- *Determine Budget – one day*
  - o *Since they've already acted on the research phase, they'll get together for a day to put the budget together and come to an agreement.*
- *Choose Wedding Colors and Themes – one day*
  This is something they'll also discuss when they have their meeting. Now if it was in the planning phase, it could take longer.
- *Choose Location – three weeks*

Greg and Mindy have already researched different locations, now it's time to call the places and take a look and ask questions. They have about five on their list. When they look at their schedule, they only have time to go to two locations a week. So, they estimate three weeks.

Step 2. Add Buffers

If you know the more accurate estimate, keep in mind to add some buffer. A buffer is adding in some extra cushion time for the unexpected. You want to do this because there's always life's unexpected curveballs. This will give you a more realistic schedule and take away your stress.

For example, Greg and Mindy estimate that it will take three weeks to find a wedding location, but they're a busy couple, and a lot of stuff can come up. If they have room in their schedule, they can estimate one month to add some buffer.

Create Milestones

Now that you have estimates for each task, let's now put them into the time categories.

- ✓ Daily – This is where you'll focus on your daily tasks.
- ✓ Monthly – This is when you'll focus in on the month.
- ✓ Quarterly – This is in three-month increments. For example: Quarter 1 is January, February, and March.

✓ Yearly – This is the bigger picture. It may take a while to accomplish this.

Hannah has a goal to start college. She has already broken down her tasks and estimated her time. She's ready to put her puzzle pieces into each timed category. Let's take a look at her timed categories for her goals.

- *This goes into her daily action schedule.*
  - o *Apply for chosen college*
  - o *Sign up for FAFSA*
  - o *Purchase books*
  - o *Start classes*
- *This goes into her weekly schedule.*
  - o *Study*
- *This goes into her yearly schedule.*
  - o *Graduate*

Once you've broken them into your timed categories, find your milestones. Milestones don't have a duration; it's when you've accomplished something worth rewarding yourself. Her milestone can be starting class and graduating. Highlight these milestones and have dates put on your calendar to work towards. Now you have the meat and potatoes, so it's time to transition this blueprint into your schedule.

Lessons

- **You need to break your goals into small pieces called tasks.**
- **Tasks are the action part you work on to help accomplish your goals.**
- **A goal can be ongoing or a project.**
- **If it's ongoing, it's more of a habit, routine, or ritual that you want to accomplish.**
- **If it's a project the goal has a beginning and an end.**
- **How to break goals down into tasks**
  - Step 1. Research
  - Step 2. Get All the Puzzle Pieces Together
- **Categorize your tasks**
  - Category 1. The Research Phase
  - Category 2. The Planning Phase
  - Category 3. The Action Phase
  - Category 4. The Review Phase
- **Prioritize your tasks**
  - Step 1. Start forwards or backwards
  - Step 2. Ranking
- **Estimate how long each task will take**
  - Step 1. Estimate your best guess
  - Step 2. Add buffers
- **Create milestones**
  - Put them into the time categories
    - Daily

➢ Monthly

➢ Quarterly

➢ Yearly

CHAPTER 8

Develop Your New Schedule

In This Chapter, I Will Help You:
- ➢ **Review your ideal schedule**
- ➢ **Understand different types of schedules**
- ➢ **Get more time in your schedule**
- ➢ **Create your new schedule**

E veryone's schedule will be different. There's no one-size-fits-all answer. We'll discuss the different types of schedules as we go through developing one. It's important to have a schedule. Otherwise, you're just responding to everything, and you can easily fall into being busy, but not productive.

If you don't have a schedule, it's hard to implement habits you want to create, goals you want to achieve, and to manage the chaos. It's like a house without a strong foundation. When the wind blows, the house can easily fall down. A schedule can be difficult to create because so many things happen. There's a lot to dissect and strategies on how to do this right for your life. Let's start with finding out what you want your ideal schedule to look like.

Create Your Ideal Schedule

Review the goals you listed in the previous chapters. This is the time where you start creating it into your schedule. When coaching friends and family, I hear a lot of the goals below.

- ✓ I want to read more.
- ✓ I want to work out more.
- ✓ I want to cook more.
- ✓ I want to spend more time with my loved ones.
- ✓ I want to study for school or a certification.
- ✓ I want to start my own business.
- ✓ I want to complete a certain project.

Once they put this into their schedules and focus on executing the task or developing the habit, they accomplish the goals. If it isn't in the schedule, then it's just a goal that sits there, waiting to be done. You become someone who just talks the talk but doesn't walk the walk.

Let's take it a step further and put a time you desire to spend time on these goals. Do you want to read thirty minutes a day? Do you want to work on your business all day Saturday? Write down what you desire. Sometimes you may not know what time you can work with until you understand your current schedule.

This is why we need to do an analysis of what your current schedule looks like. Once you understand your current schedule, we can see how much time we can carve out to add your goals in and find what's working and what's not working. There are different types of schedules we have that can determine how we design our new schedule. Let's take a look at them.

Understand Different Types of Schedules

1. **I don't have much to do in my day** - You may not have a lot of commitments and responsibilities. For this type of person, you have a lot of time in your day. The busy people can envy you. If you have a lot of goals you want to accomplish, this will be much easier to work with. We just create a specific time slots into your day. These time slots will consist of habits you want to create and tasks you want to get done.

   One of my good friends doesn't work. She was staying at home to finish her PHD program. Now that she's done, she has a lot more time on her hands. Her lifestyle can be much different from mine since I work a full-time job, I'm a mother and have many responsibilities.

   Let's say she wanted to publish a book on relationships. She commits to spending three hours a day, from four p.m. to seven p.m. to meet her deadline of publishing it in three months. For her, her default schedule will just be the time allocated for her book. She doesn't need to go into any other detail for her day unless she wants to commit to any type of goals.

2. **My schedule changes every week** – Maybe you don't have the traditional nine-to-five job. Maybe your hours fluctuate every week, and you don't know what they are until a certain day in the week. For this person, you create a schedule for the week as soon as you receive your schedule.

   I have a best friend who fits into this category. I try to schedule stuff with her way ahead of time, but it often clashes because she doesn't know her schedule until the following Saturday. For her situation, she can have a framework of what she wants to do each week. She wants to work on her business for four hours during the week, read thirty minutes a night, and spend time with God one hour in the morning. She gets her schedule at work on Saturday morning. I suggest that later on Saturday, she plans out her schedule for the rest of the week, implementing her goals. This helps her to stay organized and productive.

3. **My schedule changes every day** – Maybe you can't even predict how your day will go because it changes each day. You may be self-employed and respond immediately to your client once they call you for your services. It's hard to predict ahead of time what your default schedule will look like in these cases.

   In this case, instead of saying I want to do X from eight a.m. to nine a.m., you can have a checklist of things you want to get done in the day. If you have an idea of the time frame you want to spend, you can put that. The difference is it doesn't go into a time slot. If you don't have a time frame, and it's just a task that needs to get done, you work on it, complete it, then go to the next thing on your list.

As a project manager, my schedule changes every day. I get meeting invites all the time. I have all kinds of action items that come up throughout the day. It's vital for me to work off a list to stay organized and take care of important things. I prioritize this list and focus on one thing at a time. If I get interrupted, I handle it, then I go back to where I left off on my list.

4. **Most days of the week, my schedule is the same** – There are some people who have a similar schedule. They go to work the same time almost every day. They have the same routine when they get off work. In this situation, when scheduling your goals, you'll use time slots to put into your new schedule.

You know what available time you have outside of your current routine, and you can review what needs to change, if you need to add more things into your life. Some people can be a combination of any of these.

Now that you have a good understanding of what type of schedule you have, you can be redesigning your schedule. This could be simple for those have freer time; you simply just need to write it out and stick to it.

How To Get More Time Into Your Schedule

For those who are way too busy and don't know where you can squeeze time into your schedule, here are ways to make more time for what's important.

Tip 1. Limit or remove your commitments - It's easy for us to get overcommitted because we think we can be superman or superwomen, or we don't know how to say no. If you want more time in your schedule, you want to look at limiting or removing some of your commitments.

Some of my commitments are going to church every Sunday and coaching family and friends on achieving their goals. I had to limit my coaching to get other things done. Instead of doing it throughout the week, I only have that availability once a week. I'm okay with doing this right now since life coaching isn't my top priority.

Tip 2. Delegate your responsibilities – It's easy to get bombarded with the responsibilities of life and depending on what season you're in or cards you've been dealt, this list could be pretty big. There are creative ways to delegate your responsibilities if you want to make more time.

For me, instead of taking a few hours on my days off going to different stores and getting groceries, I delegated that work to the employees at the store. I use the grocery pickup, where the employees get the groceries for me and load it into my car. I've also used the

118

home delivery service for my groceries. This has carved out a lot of time in my schedule. I also delegate my responsibilities, whether that's to my husband, some of my teammates, or a service I pay for. Where this is a will, there's a way.

Tip 3. Eliminate Time Wasters – Do you have too much down time? I'm a big believer on having some down time. This is important to rechange and have a mental break. Sometimes, though, we go too far and become lazy or fall into the trap of time wasters. Time wasters are things you do that aren't contributing to your future. It's okay to have some of this in your life for your own sanity, but it becomes a problem when it halts your progress. Some time wasters watch too much TV, browsing through social media, playing video games, talking on the phone, lying on the couch eating potato chips all day. If you need more time in your day, find ways to cut back on your down time or eliminate it.

Create Your New Schedule

Now that you understand what you're trying to add into your schedule, the type of schedule you're working with, and how much time you can free up, let's put together your new schedule. I suggest having a daily schedule and a weekly checklist. For your daily schedule, you want to work off your default schedule.

1 Create your default schedule – A default schedule is what your day and week would look like in a perfect world of no distractions. It's the framework of you getting things done and balancing your life. You'll create this based off the different types of schedules we discussed earlier in this chapter. It's important to have this because it helps you achieve your goals.

2 Create your Daily Schedule – Your daily schedule will look just like your default schedule I just mentioned. Copy over your default schedule for the day. The only difference is, add unexpected things that come up. You may have to tweak or change what's on your schedule. This happens almost every time.

I wake up in the morning and create the schedule for my day. You can do this at night or whatever works best for you. Here's an example of some unexpected stuff that came up. My little boy got a little sick, so I needed to stop by the store and get some elderberry medicine.

Also, my best friend just told me she would like me to plan her Zoom party, but it's in two days! She's special to me, so even though I'm busy with deadlines, I want to make time to give her the best.

These are all unexpected items not on my default schedule. With a puzzled look, I think to myself, "Let's see how I can make room for these two items on today's schedule." I add getting my son's medicine during my lunch break, then I can grab some food on the go.

For my best friend, I'm wondering where I can find time to plan her party. I look at my schedule and see that I have a plan before I go to bed to read for thirty minutes. I decide just for the next two days to replace that time of reading for time to plan her birthday party.

Do you see how the default schedule was a template for me, but the daily schedule is something I need to follow for today, but accounts for the unexpected? Unexpected stuff comes up almost all the time, and that's why these two schedules work great for me. I'm not just making things up on the fly; I have a default schedule to help me stay on track with habits and also time to achieve goals. I have a daily schedule to help me focus on that day and include any important items that need to get done for the day.

3 Create your weekly checklist – A weekly checklist differs from a default or daily schedule because it's one large task that needs to be complete anytime during the week. For me, my weekly schedule is so busy, I probably won't have time to check off on my weekly checklist during the week, so I work on my checklist on Friday and the weekends. Here's an example of what my weekly checklist looks like.

Example

- ✓ **Deep clean** – This for cleaning the house. I tidy up through the week and try to do a deep clean sometime on the weekends.
- ✓ **Review my goals** – This is for reviewing my goals for the month. I have a document I save on my computer. It's almost like a journal. I have a date, and I talk about

what's working, what's not working, and what do I need to start, stop, continue, or revise. This helps me stay accountable.

✓ **Budget and pay bills** – This is where I budget and make sure I pay the bills on time.

✓ **Projects** – This is for any projects I want to complete.

You've found out what you wanted to add into your schedule based off the type of schedule you have. You've found ways to make more time in your schedule, and you created three important documents to keep you on track: your default schedule, your daily schedule, and your weekly checklist. You now have your blueprint. Let's talk about the tools to help you stay on track with implementing your blueprint.

Lessons

Create your ideal schedule

o   Review your goals: habits and projects you want to implement into your new schedule.

Understand different types of schedules

o   I don't have much to do in my day.

o   My schedule changes every week.

o   My schedule changes every day.

o   Most days of the week, my schedule is the same.

How to get more time into your schedule

o   **Tip 1.** Limit or remove your commitments.

o   **Tip 2.** Delegate your responsibilities.

o   **Tip 3.** Eliminate time wasters.

Create your new schedule

o   1. Create your default schedule.

o   2. Create your daily schedule.

o   3. Create your weekly checklist.

PART 4

◁◆▷

Let's Get Organized!

"Organization isn't about perfection;
it's about efficiency, reducing stress and clutter,
saving time and money and improving your overall quality of life."
-Christina Scalise

In Part 4...

This will be my favorite section to discuss because I simply love organizing. It could be my middle name. This is what helps the madness become bearable. It's what helps huge organizations with thousands of employees function successfully. They have processes, procedures, and other things in place. They don't just have some action items and run with it. They have tools and things to account for. When curveballs are thrown at them, they have a foundation in place, so they don't crumble.

When I run a million-dollar project, there are so many tasks to complete. It's vital to be organized in every area for the success of the project and for my own peace of mind. This is what many people are missing. They can have the roadblocks removed, have the blueprint, have a schedule, but they don't have the right tools to build the vision, so they'll struggle.

In Part 4, I talk about finding a home for everything, whether you're using technology or paper. I explain important tools you need to have to succeed. I also talk about the importance of having a master list and how to use it correctly to manage all your tasks.

CHAPTER 9

Get Organized

‚‚

In This Chapter, I Will Tell You:

➢ **Why it's important to find a home for everything**

➢ **The benefits of paper versus technology**

➢ **Some items to get your hands on that will set you up for success**

‚‚

When designers plan work on a house, they need all the tools, parts, and skills to actually create it. You don't want to go ice skating in your bathing suit, right? That's what I mean when I say you need the necessary tools to succeed.

Let's start off with the right tools you need to manage the chaos.

Paper Versus Technology?

One important question to ask yourself is paper versus technology when using documents and tools for organization. Do you like to feel of the pen in your hand as you cross things out? Are you not good at using technology? Then, it may be best for you to use paper.

One of my sisters is still learning how to use technology. It can be stressful trying to learn all these tools. Unless she takes a class or finds way to learn, it would be less stressful for her just to use paper.

Are you tech savvy? Do you prefer everything in one easy space? Do you hate to write? Then, technology is best for you. If you know how to use technology, it can be beneficial and make things quicker, but it's all about what works best for you.

My husband is a senior programmer. He's one hundred percent a technology guy. He doesn't like paper. It's best for him to use all technology resources to keep him organized.

Are you a little of both? Then you can try a combination of both. I started off using paper a lot. Then my husband showed me cool tools using technology, so I gravitated towards that. I still do both, but mainly technology.

Find what feels best for you, by using trial and error. Just as everyone has different interests and hobbies, not all are alike. This isn't a cookie cutter, simply a guideline. Follow the concepts as well as the recommendations to find what you like.

Once you've determined what format works best for you, it's time to get into using different tools.

Filing Systems

You need a home for everything. Stuffing everything into a drawer with no type of organization isn't filing done correctly. There will be times when you need to look for important items. Having a place for everything keeps you organized, less stressed, and more successful. We'll talk about some tools you can use to file with technology and tools to use that you'll need for filing in your home or workplace.

Filing with Technology

You need to find a home for any items you'll save on the computer. Many of your documents will be saved with Microsoft Suite items: Microsoft Word, Excel, PowerPoint, PDF, Visio, and more. You can also use pictures, videos, and music, etc.

 ## Recommendations

1. **Save your information on a cloud.** A cloud is a storage model that saves your data over the internet. If your computer crashes, you don't lose everything because it's on a cloud. You don't want to learn the hard way. Now, if you have some important documents, you can also use an external hard drive backup.

   Some clouds I recommend are Google Drive, Dropbox, or OneDrive. I've used all of them in the past. For the last five years, I currently use OneDrive. This is also on my desktop. I like the many options they have for notes and the layout.

2. **Have folder types saved in your folder.** In your cloud, you can create any of the folders that are applicable to you. I like

to have one for each year and just copy over important files into the next year.

Folder Labels

➢ **Spiritual** – If you have any programs, you can create folders for this. I also have documents for declarations, people I want to pray for, Scripture. Anything spiritually related can go into this folder.

➢ **Family** – In the family folder, you can have a subfolder for events. This is where you can put vacations that you plan, events that you need to organize, any children's activities or social gatherings, etc. You can also have one for each member of the family. For example, I have a subfolder for my son. Then, in that folder, I have another sub-folder for his school since he's working virtually. Any documents I need to save will go in there.

➢ **Health** – In the health folder, I have saved PDFs of recipes or important health information. I've created Excel documents for working out. I also have meal planning. You can create sub folders for fitness and nutrition.

➢ **Finances** – In my finance folder, I have included our budget, the due dates of our bills, my checks and balances sheet.

➢ **Career/Business** – You can put any work-related items in here. I've put my resume, cover letter, documents from my job, business items, etc.

➢ **Goals** – This is where you can have your weekly checklist that you'll review. You can have your trajectory, monthly goals, etc.

➢ **Photos** – A folder for photos.

➢ **Other** – For anything else, customize what works for you.

Finding a Home for Everything

Now that you have your filing system set up on your computer, let's get it set up in your home. Having a filing system at home can make a huge difference and can be rewarding. It feels good to have all your items in place and takes the headache out of finding things and just looks better. Let's take a look at five items you need.

1. **A letter tray** – During the week, you may have  paperwork, receipts, mail, sticky notes, things you wrote down as they come to you. As you're moving quickly through your week, you need a temporary holding place for all these documents. Sometimes you get too busy to put them up. This is where you'll get a box. You can do the same thing at work.

In your weekly routine, you'll choose a day to empty out this box and file them. Depending on what you have, it can take anywhere from five to fifteen minutes to unload. You sit down and start to sort them into different places. One can go into an important folder, junk box, trash, and any other items you've designated. We'll discuss some of these.

2. **A file storage box, file folder, or filing cabinet** – This

 box is important to have all your papers you need to keep. Inside of this box, you'll need different folders with individual labels, which

can be titled as the following:

- ✓ Important
- ✓ Copies
- ✓ Car Information
- ✓ Stuff for your kids / Medical / etc.
- ✓ Memories
- ✓ Income Tax
- ✓ Stuff to keep
- ✓ Business / Career
- ✓ You can create other labels customized for your life.

Then, anytime you unload your box during your weekly time slot, you can put those documents in the designated folder. You have everything you need, and anytime you're looking for something you, can easily find it.

3. **A zipper binder with a folder inside, a safety box, or a safe -**

For this, you'll save important information. This would be your warranty deed for your house, marriage license, birth certificates, and social security cards.

4. **An office compartment**

For an office compartment, you can put documents closer to you with folders that you look at on a consistent basis. This may be a project you're working on and other items. I've used this a lot at work.

5. **A storage ottoman** – For a storage ottoman, you can put

a bunch of stuff. I recommend only putting information here that you may need in the future, but probably won't. It's just something you don't want to throw away, but you may one day look at. If it gets full, over time you can clean it out to see if you still need it or not.

Important Tools to Have

Now that you have a home for all your items, it's time to look at some important tools that you need. We'll review the calendar, the planner, and a tool to remind you of important items. These tools keep all your stuff organized and keep you on track.

1. **A calendar** – If you want to go down the technology route, you can use the calendar on your phone or through Microsoft Outlook. I'm sure there are plenty of other applications you can use, too. If you want to do it via paper, you can buy a calendar that you can take with you wherever you go. You can have a desktop calendar laying on your desk, one hanging up, or even one on your fridge. Use the one you know you'll look at a lot. I've had all them.

   A calendar is to be used for timed events such as birthdays and meetings. You can also add in important items that you need to do. I like to use my calendar on my phone for events and the calendar on my fridge.

   For example, someone tells you last minute that they have a birthday party in a few days. You say, "Okay, I'll be there," and don't even write it down. When you get home, you get slammed with all kinds of new things that come up and before you know it, it's time to go to bed.

   You wake up rushing to get to work, you had to stay overtime, and by the time you get home, you're exhausted. You're excited that the next day is the weekend. Before you go to bed, you panic because you realize it's your friend's birthday party the next day. You're glad you remembered, but you still have to get a gift, and you don't have any time in the morning before the party. You now have to figure it out. This could have been avoided if you put it in your calendar.

2. **A planner** – A lot of your planning, brainstorming, organizing, and information can be held in a planner. This is where you do the work. If you have a specific project or event, you can use your planner to break down all the tasks for that specific item. Someone asks you to host a Christmas party at your house. You can use your planner to write down everything you need to get it done.

You can buy a planner at the store or use software. I love using OneNote. I heard OneNote is similar to Evernote. I use OneNote on a daily basis. I have several projects. I love the way it's laid out, has different notebooks and subpages. It helps me to easily organize different areas of my life.

3. **A tool to remind you** – Another important tool is to have a way to remind you of things. It's one thing to write everything down, but what if you forget to look at it? I use my reminder application often. There are different ways to trigger you to remember to do something.

A guy at my job loved using sticky notes. He had it all over his computer, so it was difficult for him to forget something. I've used that before, and I would put the sticky note in front of something I knew I couldn't miss.

I've heard of people texting themselves, leaving a voicemail, or an email. My husband likes to use the calendar in his phone. He sets the reminder ahead of the event he has scheduled. If it isn't specifically in the calendar, he'll just push a button on his phone, speak, and the reminder is set up.

I like to use an application on my phone called, "To Do Reminder." It's so simple. Anytime I need an important reminder for the day, I just put what it is and set the time. I'll do that for simple stuff. Like for today, the store is scheduled to drop off my groceries at the door at eleven a.m. I set that as a reminder, so the alarm will go off and remind me. This prevents me from missing them and having unattended groceries left on my porch.

Since I've been working at home a lot and not going anywhere, sometimes I just add the reminder on my daily schedule because I'm constantly looking at it. Whatever you choose, make sure it'll be something that works. Having this tool will prevent you from letting anything slip through cracks and be better prepared.

Lessons

Choose what works best for you: paper, technology, or both.

Tips for filing with technology:

- o   Save your information on a cloud.
- o   Have folder types saved in your folder.

Find a home for everything.

- o   A letter tray
- o   A file storage box, file folder, or filing cabinet
- o   A zipper binder with a folder inside of it, a safety box, or safe
- o   An office compartment
- o   A storage ottoman

Important tools to have.

- o   A calendar
- o   A planner
- o   A reminder tool

CHAPTER 10

Managing Your Master List

In This Chapter, I Discuss:

- ➢ Having a temporary holding spot for your tasks
- ➢ How to create your Master List

Tasks are always popping up, and they almost never go away. They're the action items you complete that move you towards your goals. When you learn to manage them with structure in different areas of your life, you accomplish your goals one after another.

If you don't have a system to manage your tasks, chaos can form. This will cause stress, being overwhelmed, forgetting important things, and overall slow you down or stop you from reaching your full potential.

 ## Have a Temporary Holding Place for Your Tasks

A lot of times, we go throughout our day and suddenly think of all these things we need to do. I need to withdraw some money out of the bank. I need to stop by my aunt's this weekend and see how she's doing. I need to research how to invest. Oh, I need to plan this meal for the upcoming holiday. This list goes on and on.

Another thing that can often happen is unexpected requests from people. People ask, "Can you help me with my resume?" "Can you call me back in the evening?" "Can you give me some game ideas for the holidays?" This list can also grow quickly. I see this a lot in my life and in the corporate world.

If you don't want to forget things or feel like a chicken with its head cut off, don't make the mistake of what some people do, and not write things down that come up throughout your day. I realized that a lot of organized people already have the habit of jotting everything down in one place, so it isn't all floating in their heads. They understand that they need to use that mental capacity for other important items.

You need a temporary holding place for your tasks. This is especially helpful if you're busy or out somewhere. A temporary holding place can be a small notebook you carry with you or even an application on your phone. Anytime you think of something you need to do or someone asks you to do something, I don't care how simple it is, write it down.

I have two temporary holding places. My first one is a whiteboard on the side of my fridge. I use this for any food or household items that I need to get when I go grocery shopping later that week. I start thinking, "Oh no, we're out of paper bowls." "Uh oh, looks like we need to get more rice." "Man, I'm already out of black pepper." When I find what I need to get that week, I just walk over to the fridge and write it down. This works well for me.

My second temporary holding place is a simple phone application I use called A Note. Any tasks that I think of throughout the day or that come up from other people, I take a few seconds and add it into my A Note and then keep going on about my day.

The Master List

Now that I have a temporary holding place, I need to transfer everything to the end destination, my master list. I recommend transferring everything no longer than a week. If you can do it sooner, that's great. Let's talk about what a master list is, why it's important, and how to use it the right way.

A master list is basically a brain dump of all tasks you need to complete. Depending on how busy you are, this list can be small to long. You can have your master list be on a piece of paper, your planner, or a Microsoft product like Excel or Word on your computer.

The reason we separate a temporary holding place and a master list is because sometimes you're on the go and can't get to your master list, so you use the holding place. This happens a lot. If you always stay at home, then you may not use the temporary holding place very much and can skip straight to the master list.

Another reason we separate them is the master list can easily grow. It's a list of tasks from your past, your goals, and things that come up throughout the day. If you're busy, it's hard to get everything done, and I don't recommend you trying unless they're all priorities.

I've been there and done that, and I realize that I can't spend my entire week just trying to get every task done. Instead, I focus on priorities; the other stuff can come when the time gets there. This will help you stay organized and not miss a beat.

 # How to Create Your Master List

Creating your master list can be simple. Use a piece of paper, your planner, or take it up a notch and use it on your computer. There are many ways to do it. Find what suits you best. I've done them all. Using Excel and Microsoft Word works best for me. I normally use Excel, but if my list grows way out of hand, I like to use Microsoft word.

How to Work Off Your Master List

There are different ways you can use your master list, and it depends on your style. Some people just have the list of tasks in no particular order or category. It's just one long list. I do this sometimes when I just have way too many things to do.

Tip 1. If you have just one long list, I recommend skimming through the tasks and find the ones that need to be done today. Highlight them, write the word "next" beside them, do something to make those tasks stand out. This will signal you to only focus on these tasks. You can also highlight a different color for the ones that are due soon, so you can focus on those next. Then just work off all the ones highlighted.

Tip 2. If you want to be a little more organized, arrange that list of tasks into categories. This could make things less overwhelming when you see a long list. For example, I have categories for home life, finances, business, projects, events, and others. I place the tasks under the appropriate category.

Tip 3. If you want to go a step further and be even more organized and fancy, next to each task, you could put the type of effort it will take and when they're due. For type of urgency, I keep it simple. If it takes me five minutes or less, give or take, I consider it a low level. It doesn't take much brain power. You can do the lower-level items when you want to get a lot done at once, are pressed for time, or your energy is low.

If it takes more time and more brain power, I consider it a higher level. You can work on the higher-level items when you have more time, more energy, or want to knock out the hard stuff in the beginning of your day.

Lessons

Have a temporary holding place for your tasks

- o Use a small notebook
- o Use an application on your phone

Transfer your tasks

- o Transfer your tasks from your temporary holding place to your master list

Master list

- o A master list is a home for all of your tasks at any given time.
- o A master list can be a piece of paper, your planner, or a Microsoft Suite document like Word or Excel.

Work off your master list

- o Tip 1. If you just want one long list, I suggest highlighting all the ones due today and do another color for the ones due soon.
- o Tip 2. If you want to go a step further, I suggest categorizing the tasks.
- o Tip 3. If you want to be more organized and fancier, I suggest putting the due date next to each task and the type of effort it will take.
  - ➤ Lower-Level: A task that takes up to five to ten minutes and doesn't require a lot of brain power.
  - ➤ Higher-Level: A task that takes more than ten minutes and requires a lot of brain power.

PART 5

Staying Consistent

In Part 5...

Congratulations, you've come so far. You removed roadblocks in your way, you found out what you want out of life, and created a blueprint for it, then you created a schedule where you're working on your goals, and you have the tools in place. Before you know it, you'll be knocking goals out one by one. But we all know that life throws us some crazy curve balls.

You can have great momentum, but then stuff happens. You want to make sure that you finish what you start. That you see the fruit of your labor.

In Part 5, I talk about how to handle different distractions, both external and internal. Then, I'll give you several rules to live by, discuss how to beat procrastination, and talk about the importance of knowing the price you'll pay upfront. Once you've learned these concepts, you'll be a person who masters goal after goal, living the life you've always wanted.

CHAPTER 11

Dealing with Distractions

In This Chapter, I Will Teach You:
  - ➢ **How to handle external distractions**
  - ➢ **How to deal with internal distractions**

Maybe you were off to a great start, but you got distracted along the way, or something unexpected happened. Where do you go from here? It's best to be fully prepared by being proactive, so you can bounce back anytime life throws you a surprise. We'll discuss how to handle external distractions and deal with internal distractions. External distractions are anything that happens outside of you.

Internal distractions are what's happening on the inside of you.

External Distractions

Olivia was doing great on tackling her goals, but after a month, she found herself way too distracted, so she slacked off and lost motivation. When we review her distractions, we notice she has a lot of external distractions.

Your Environment – *Olivia has been trying to do a lot of her actions at night. Her husband and kids require a lot of*

145

attention during that time. Her environment is loud and very distracting. She knows she can't control that because she's a wife and mother and doesn't want to neglect that area.

 Tip: Sometimes it's simply shifting the time you do things to better control your environment. If there are a lot of distractions, you can wake up early when everyone is asleep to get things done, or you can wait till everyone goes to bed. Choose when you're most alert. Also, the space you're in plays a part. Do you need to go to a library? Do you have an office? Can you do it on your lunch at work? Understand that places can give off energy. For example, you may be more motivated working out in the gym than at home. If you can't control the time and place, try to be creative. Olivia decides to put on some headphones and schedule a better time.

Technology – *Olivia notices that her phone is always ringing during the times she tries to be productive. She looks up, and an hour has already gone by. She also notices that every time she gets an email notification, she stops her work to check them.*

Tips

> ➤ **Phone Calls** – Technology can be a big distraction. We receive consistent phone calls, emails, and even get stuck internet surfing. These can be time suckers if you allow it. If you have a time block to accomplish some important tasks, and the phone rings, you can call that person back.

You can either not answer, send them a text saying I'll call you back, or answer the phone and say hi and tell them what you're doing, and you'll call back. I find that some people don't get the hint, so if possible, I would steer clear of answering.

Of course, if it's an emergency, you can answer and adjust. Treat your time like you're at a job. Otherwise, you won't get your stuff done, or it will take a much longer time.

➤ **Emails** – As for emails, you don't have to answer them every time it comes in. This goes especially for work, unless of course that's your job. If you don't have down time, have time blocks set up for when you look at email. If you have time, then feel free to respond or at least categorize them.

Categorize Your E-mails

In Microsoft Outlook, you can categorize and color code follow ups, action items, and add notes. There are plenty more, but you can start with these. That way you aren't pressured to act right then. You can have a system for these categories.

✓ **Follow ups** – These are things you're waiting on from someone. If you haven't heard back, you follow up. I often like to blind-copy myself and keep that categorized email until it's resolved, then I file it away. This helps me make sure nothing falls through the cracks.

✓ **Action items** – This can help you flag things you need to get done. You can keep that email there until it has been done.

✓ **Add notes** is just an email with information. That information needs to be transferred to one of the documents I created. Since I have these categories in place, I can categorize them and get back to them when I'm available.

➢ **Social Media** – *Another external distraction Olivia faces is social media. She often likes to go through her newsfeed on Facebook and Instagram. She wants to know how her family and friends are doing. The problem is that the thirty minutes she could have been focusing on her goals has now been eaten up by mindless browsing.*

A lot of people get sucked into browsing on social media, whether that's Facebook, Instagram, Snapchat, Twitter, and many more. You just need to limit your time doing this. You can do it on your breaks, when you're relaxing, but don't do it when you're trying to get things done.

➢ **Netflix Binge Watching** – *Another external distraction Olivia faces is she likes to watch Netflix on her days off. It's okay for her to relax, but she also has a lot of action items to do on her days off. Sometimes she uses that time to binge-watch shows on Netflix.*

This can happen to the best of us, no matter how disciplined we are. Since these can be addicting, I try to stay away from it during the week. On the weekends, I may watch an episode, then work on tasks, then repeat.

If I'm busy, I may watch an episode for ten minutes, accomplish some tasks, and then repeat. Another option would be to watch the shows during the time I work out on the treadmill. You can get creative. The point is you don't want TV to consume all your time. So, if you don't want to eliminate it, then limit it. You can reward yourself with these shows but just make sure to find room to get your action items done.

The Unexpected – *There are some external distractions that Olivia can control, but what about the things she cannot? Sometimes she faces the unexpected and gets way too many interruptions.*

This is something you should account for when developing your schedule. This is why you add a buffer to add flexibility to your schedule. When an interruption happens, sometimes it will be eaten up, but you're still on track because you added buffer. This is what we do in the project management world when we create schedules. We add wiggle room because we know unexpected things come up.

Tip: Create Back-up Schedules – *Creating a backup schedule can also be useful.*

One goal of Olivia's is to run outdoors three times a week. If the weather is bad, Olivia will go to the gym. If she's running short on time, she will run for less time. If she can't work out the day she planned, she has a backup day.

Since Olivia has these backup plans when the unexpected comes, she simply shifts her schedule, but she's still on track with her goals. If all else fails, and she had a bad week, she picks herself up from where she was and keeps going. No need to beat yourself up. Life isn't linear.

Toxic People – *One last distraction Olivia faces is she has some toxic friends in her life. She doesn't even know why she's still friends with them. When she's around them, they bring her down and suck up her energy. She must be careful who she lets into her life. If she wants to go far, she needs to trim out people who don't add value to her life, but do the complete opposite. She needs to surround herself with people who are encouraging, motivating, and people who can help her be accountable.*

If she has no one, she can start with being that to herself. Olivia decides to let go of toxic friends and the toxic family members she just loves from a distance. Now that Olivia has discovered her external distractions and either limited them or removed them, she's back on track with her goals.

Internal Distractions

What about distractions that come from within? This can include your mind and emotions.

Paula is trying to work on her goal to go to a beauty college. She had all her plans and was ready to execute them, but something unexpected happened to her. Out of nowhere, she found out her fiancé was cheating on her, and he broke up with her. She's depressed, discouraged, and becoming more and more unmotivated. She doesn't want to eat or get out of bed.

Internal distractions can be very tough to deal with when you're dealing with storms in your life. It's important to have practical steps in place to help you stay on track. You can still have a goal going on and be working through some stuff.

Paula decides to do something about her depression.

 # Tips to Handle Internal Distractions

1. **Confide in a trusted friend** – She schedules some time to confide in a trusted friend to help talk about what she's going through. This helps her to not try to dissect what just happened or figure things out by herself right now.

2. **Write in a journal** – If she has a flood of thoughts that she can't ignore, she gets a journal to get her thoughts out. This helps her connect to her thoughts and get it out of her system.

3. **Take a break** – She takes a weekend trip and relaxes with nature. She watches her favorite show, eats her favorite meal, and gets some good rest. She also watches videos on motivation and reminds herself why she's working towards her vision.

4. **See a therapist** – She tells herself she'll see a therapist if she can't get it together. It's important to find ways to bounce back. Some things take time, so take one step at a time. A therapist helps her dig deep, communicate, pour things out, and heal.

5. **Pray** – She always stays in prayer; she knows that prayer moves mountains.

Internal distraction can happen any time and can really halt your progress if you let it. When I wrote this book, I had some unexpected personal information come to me. It scrambled my brain, and finishing my book was the last thing on my mind. I followed most of the steps above and was able to bounce back. I realized I couldn't stay where I was.

"Even if you are on the right track, you'll get run over if you just sit there."

-Will Rogers

Lessons

It's best to be fully prepared by being proactive so you can bounce back anytime life throws you a surprise.

External distractions are anything that happens outside of you.

Internal distractions are what's happening on the inside of you.

External distractions

- o Your environment
  - ➢ Shift the time you do things.
  - ➢ Wake up early when everyone is asleep or wait until everyone goes to bed.
  - ➢ Change your environment into the atmosphere you want.
  - ➢ If you can't do anything, put on headphones.
- o Technology
  - ➢ Phone calls
    - Tell them you'll call them back.
    - Don't answer unless it's an emergency.
    - Send them a text and tell them you'll call them back.
    - Treat your time like you're at a job.
  - ➢ E-mails
    - Don't answer them every time it comes in, unless it's your job.
    - Have time blocks set up.
    - Categorize your emails, then get back to them
- o Follow ups
- o Action items

o Add notes

> Social Media (Facebook, Instagram, Snapchat, Twitter, etc.)

• You can do this on your breaks or when you're relaxing, but don't do it when you're trying to get things done.

> Shows

• Try it just on your days off.

• If you're busy, do a task after an episode or every ten mins.

• You can watch it while on the treadmill.

o The Unexpected

> Create back-up schedules

o Toxic People

> Let go of toxic friends and family members, love them from a distance.

▪ Internal Distractions

o Tips to Handle Internal Distractions

> Confide in a trusted friend

> Write in a journal

> Take a break

> See a therapist

> Pray

CHAPTER 12

Rules to Live By

‘‘

In This Chapter, I Will Give You:
  ➢ **Rules to live by to stay the course**
  ➢ **Advice on how to overcome procrastination**

‘‘

I f you want to remain consistent, there are some rules you need to follow. If you don't follow these, you're setting yourself up for failure. The first is getting adequate sleep. You can have everything you need to succeed, but if you aren't giving your body proper sleep, you won't be able to function.

 The Rules of The Game

1. **Make getting enough sleep a priority** – It's like a drunk driver: why is that person even driving drunk? What's the point of trying to focus if you feel like a zombie? You need to make sleep a priority if you want to be consistent. Take care of the basics first, and don't cheat yourself. Get seven or eight hours of sleep each night. Move other things out of your schedule. If you have a hard time going to sleep, see a doctor. If you're currently sleep deprived, catch up on your sleep so you can get it together.

I will tell you now that, without adding this rule to my life, I wouldn't succeed. My brain would be shut down.

2. **Make sure you give yourself time to recharge** – You need breaks. Just like when a phone is about to die, it needs to be charged so it can function at its best. No matter how busy I've gotten, I make time for this. You don't want to be burned out.

   When I ran track, I did a two-mile relay. We're taught to pace ourselves until we get to the end, then give it all we have. One time, I ran hard from the very beginning, ignoring the rule of pacing myself. By the time I got close to the end, my body literally shut down, and the people behind me ran right past me with flying colors. I could have won if I had paced myself.

Tip. Have a rest day – There's a reason God rested on the seventh day, and there's a reason we have days off. Take a break, take up a hobby. It's actually more beneficial when you take your breaks since you're more productive afterwards versus pushing and pushing yourself.

This was something I learned along the way. There was a time I didn't allow for breaks. After I implemented them, I could tell a huge difference. It's like getting much-needed oil in your car, it works better. I felt revived and happier. I realized my list would always be there; it would always grow, so might as well stop trying to force myself to finish it. I just prioritize and make sure I recharge.

When I get off work, I take time to reboot. On most of my Friday evenings, I watch my favorite show and do things I love. I use Saturday for family days, and if I have some free time to knock out a couple of tasks, I'll do that. Make time for what you love! You'll always be busy; that task list will always be there, but don't wait until it's done. I've mastered so many things and still have taken my breaks.

3. **Make sure your health is in order** – If your body is struggling internally, it will be harder for you to stay working at the task. You'll feel lethargic, sick, stressed, and all kinds of things that can come up when you're in bad health. Take time to find a healthy regimen that works for you and your body. When you're eating healthy, the way you were intended to, you're more alert, you feel great, you have energy, strength, and feel amazing.

4. **Remove toxic thoughts, people, and things** – What you put out, you receive back. What you allow in your life will rub off on you. Set yourself up for success by weeding out anything that brings you down.

5. **Learn to say no and have healthy boundaries** – Don't try to be superman and superwoman, as you'll only leave yourself unhappy, drained, and taken advantage of. Sometimes you can't do something, and you can't please everybody. It's okay

to say no sometimes and have healthy boundaries and not feel guilty. You have to teach people what you will and won't allow. One key thing people in successful partnerships say is that saying no helped their relationship.

A good book on helping you learn to say no is, "The Power of a Positive No: How to Say No and Still Get to Yes," by William Ury. This book will teach you the strategy on how to say no by uncovering your yes. The strategies will help you not offend the other party, and it will help set your boundaries.

During the worst times of the pandemic, I was concerned to go out because my son was at high risk. I didn't want to jeopardize his health. There were a lot of events I got invited to. Weddings, baby showers, birthdays, and even funerals. It was extremely hard for me to say no, but I knew why I was doing it and learned how to say it. Instead of saying yes, giving a hard no, or not communicate at all. Although I know they wanted me there, they understood, and I felt good about my decision.

6. **Make sure you're doing what makes your heart sing** – You must make sure that what you're doing is what you want to do, not what others want you to do. God will put the desire in your heart, and it should make your heart sing. It should bring you joy if you're doing what you love.

7. **Have an anchor** – Find what keeps you together during the hard times. What can you hold on to, to help you through? Do

you have a role model, a good support system, or a promise you made to yourself?

My anchor has always been Jesus. I know what it feels like when I don't have Him in my life. My world was crumbling before my eyes. When I did come to help, it made a world of difference. When times get tough, He's my anchor. He's the glue that keeps me together. I would have never gotten this far without Him.

He opens doors that no man can shut. He has transformed my entire life, turning it from ashes to beauty. I know several people who have personally come to know Him, and their lives have never been the same. Having an encounter with Him changes you.

Whitney, one of my co-workers, would come to work depressed all the time. She was on antidepressant medication for years. She didn't go into details about her life, but she did tell me she wasn't sure about this whole God thing. If she did believe in Him, she would be angry at Him.

Over time, she asked me why I was so happy all the time. She said there was a glow about me. I told her about my life and what God had done for me. She was amazed at how I overcame the struggles with God's help.

I eventually left that job and a few years later, I looked at my social media and saw her. She's a totally different person. She's so happy, she's glowing, and she's talking all about what God has done for her. You can literally see the changes in her life. I touched base with her, and she wasn't the same person I had known. She had found her anchor.

8. **Get rid of bad habits** – Bad habits reap bad results. You think you're doing everything right, but you're allowing poison into your life. Determine what your unhelpful habits are and find better ones to replace them. Set yourself up for success.

   To learn more about habits, read, "The Power of Habit: Why we do what we do in life and Business," by Charles Duhigg. One thing I enjoyed about the book was when it said to create a habit, you first need a cue, like a trigger. Then it follows with a routine and a reward.

   I would always forget to do stuff until I implemented this process. For example, if I needed to sign something but had to make a run, I would put the pen on the keyboard. That pen was a trigger to remind me, so when I got back to the computer, I would sign the papers. Time can also be a trigger. For example, lunch time is my trigger to work out, and the reward is happiness. That's much better than a random time.

9. **Learn to delegate** – Don't try to do everything yourself. Have people help you. Some people think they have it all together, but don't let others do it. That's where they go wrong. Delegate, but do it wisely. Don't just give tasks to anyone; find those who are good at what they do and delegate that task to them. Give them everything they need to succeed. Give

them a deadline, and as time grows closer, get confirmation from them.

When you delegate, don't be a micromanager. Don't be bossy or pushy but be accountable and firm. I know so-called leaders who delegate wrong. There's an art in delegating and getting the best results. I've learned that in my profession as a project manager. Your team is what gets the work done for you, but if you're being a tyrant, you don't motivate them, and you may not get the result in time or the best quality.

A polite reminder well in advance is sufficient. "Hey, just following up on task A due 05/19. Please let me know if you have any concerns with that date or if you need anything from me." In this message, you're reminding them, so they're kept accountable. You're asking them to communicate with you if there are concerns and letting them know you're there to help in any way you can.

10. **Have a do it now attitude** – Stop saying I'll do it tomorrow. Woody Allen says eighty percent of your success is showing up. Things happen through actions. There will be some days you don't feel like doing it, but it's when you do the things you don't feel like doing, you're rewarded. You'll find it was well worth it.

11. **Be flexible** – Relax with the perfectionism. Things will never be perfect. Monkey wrenches will be thrown into the mix.

Loosen up and allow for flexibility. Add buffers and laugh at the things you can't control. Bounce back. Don't try to get everything done at once. The list will always be there. Focus on prioritizing and doing what you can and being okay with that. Then the next day, repeat.

12. **Manage your energy** – Remember what your body clock is. Are you a night person or morning person? A night person is most alert late at night. They go to sleep very late. When they wake up, it takes them time to reboot. They aren't very talkative when they first wake up.

For morning people, they get tired around eight or nine at night. Their brain just shuts down. They start to slur their words. They like to wake up early around five a.m., give or take, and they can jump out of bed, be talkative, and get a lot done. Find which one you are. When you're most alert, do the complicated activities. When you're tired, do the least impact activities. Follow your natural rhythm.

My husband is the night owl, and I'm the morning person. I have tried to do things late at night and well, it doesn't go well. I remember a friend asked me to write a journal article for her. I tried writing it late at night even though my brain was almost checked out. The next morning, I came up with another idea, and it was so good. I compared what I wrote at night to what I wrote in the morning, and it was totally different.

13. **Do the big tasks first** – In consideration of your body clock, do the things you don't want to do but need to do from your to-do list. Pushing it off to the very last minute will most likely set yourself up for not wanting to do it. "Eat that Frog," by Brian Tracy talks about this.

    I don't like to clean. I find when I schedule to do it later in the day, it almost never gets done. If I do it first thing in the morning, it gets done. At work, the important time-consuming tasks, I used to put at the end and would struggle to finish it; so much other stuff came up, or I didn't feel like doing it. When I put it in the beginning of my day, I was always successful in getting it done.

14. **Go with your learning style** – Everyone has different learning styles: some are visual, some are tactical, some are audio. Visual learners learn by images. They like pictures. Tactical learners learn by using their hands, through experience, or doing things. Audio learners learn best by what they hear.

    Whatever task you're doing, match it with your learning style. I'm a visual learner. I find watching videos when I want to learn something makes a huge difference versus doing it a different way. You were designed a certain way for a reason, so follow your strengths.

15. Avoid procrastination – It's easy to fall into procrastination. If you're in the habit of falling in this trap, you need to understand why you're in this place and how to avoid it.

Reasons for Procrastination

1. **You don't know what you want.** If you don't know what you want, or where you're going, then it's easy to fall prey to procrastination.

2. **You don't have anything to drive you.** You need to see the big picture, the vision. If you don't have that, when times get hard, you don't have a purpose to push you through the storms.

3. **You're settling.** You aren't aiming high enough. Your goals may be too low. You need to stretch yourself, shoot for the stars. Please don't settle. I was tempted to settle in many areas of my life, especially in relationships and my career, but I refused to settle and therefore, I got the best.

Tip: Stretch Yourself – If you aren't careful, society can try to limit you. You have to believe in yourself enough to break through those limits and not settle. If your goal is to get through the next hour instead of becoming the best you can be, it may not be as motivating. Stretch yourself.

4. **You're overwhelmed.** You'll come to a point in your life where you have way too much going on. You'll feel like you

just want to freeze because you're about to burst. This can definitely cause you not to want to do anything.

I remember the feeling of driving home after work with my body so tense that I couldn't breathe. I was that overwhelmed. I would come home with barely enough energy to make dinner. I thought to myself, "How in the world can I focus on my goals or time with my own family?" I would just pass out on the couch, with my body all tense, and I would cry. I just couldn't do it all. I remember hearing a whisper from God in the midst of my stress. He said, "You're meant to master this."

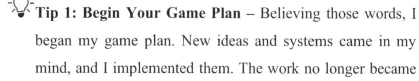 **Tip 1: Begin Your Game Plan** – Believing those words, I began my game plan. New ideas and systems came in my mind, and I implemented them. The work no longer became overwhelming to me. If God gave it to you in this season, and you know He did, then you were meant to master it and not be defeated. It's time to push back on the lies, on the negative thinking, and master this once and for all.

Tip 2: Take a break – In the meantime, take some time to unplug. Take a break. Watch your favorite show, exercise, go out with a friend. Just take a break from thinking about it. Eat your favorite food, meditate, pray. Then, come back when you've recharged and come up with a strategy.

5. **You made it a part of your identity** – Another reason for procrastination is because you believe it's who you are. You

say, "I'm just lazy. I just can't. I don't ever have time." Have you listened to the words you've told yourself lately, like really listened? You have to understand how powerful words are and how you see yourself.

Tip: It's all about how you see yourself – How you see yourself will be a reflection of how you appear to others.. So, until that changes, nothing else will. Change your narrative. You need to learn how to be optimistic and not dwell too much on the past.

6. **You're a people pleaser.** You're always trying to please people. Please learn this now, people pleasing is like a dog chasing its tail. You'll wear yourself out and be unhappy doing this. The happiest people know how to balance. They know how to say no. It isn't bad, it's saying yes to your happiness. Remember that.

7. **You're dealing with depression.** You could be depressed. This is something a lot of us can relate to. We have to fix that emotional state so we can move forward. That's why you want to do something that makes you come alive, something that brings you joy. It's also good to seek help, whether that's a psychiatrist or a trusted friend.

8. **You have low self-esteem.** You think you're not deserving enough. If you have low self-esteem and no belief in who you are, then you can feel you aren't worthy to do something great. You have to realize God has fearfully and wonderfully made you in His image. He created you for great things.

There's no one else in the world just like you. There's something special you bring into this world, and the world needs you. You have to realize just how amazing you are. Yes, you!

9. **You're just lazy**. I get it. Some days I just want to be glued to the couch all day and not do anything. Sometimes it's because you just want to relax and enjoy yourself. Other times it's because of bad health that causes you to be lethargic. Other times it's just because it can be so easy to not do the hard stuff. It's so comfortable just being in your pajamas chilling at home. I don't think anyone can argue with me on that. It's okay to have those times, you're human. The problem is when you have it so much, it becomes a hindrance to your goals.

 Tip: Push through the laziness – The beauty in birthing your dreams is it's the opposite of easy. I mean I'm sure all the mothers would love it if we could just pop a baby out without any pain. Better yet, not have to go through the nine-month process? Thanks a lot, Eve. So, sometimes you must push through your laziness to get some results. When you see them, it can motivate you to stay off that lazy bum except on the days you relax.

Lessons

If you want to stay consistent, there are some rules you need to follow.

- o **Rule 1.** Make getting enough sleep a priority.
- o **Rule 2.** Make sure you give yourself time to recharge.
- o **Rule 3.** Make sure your health is in order.
- o **Rule 4.** Remove toxic thoughts, people, and things.
- o **Rule 5.** Learn to say no and have healthy boundaries.
- o **Rule 6.** Make sure you're doing what makes your heart sing.
- o **Rule 7.** Have an anchor.
- o **Rule 8.** Get rid of bad habits.
- o **Rule 9.** Learn to delegate.
- o **Rule 10.** Have a do it now attitude.
- o **Rule 11.** Be flexible.
- o **Rule 12.** Manage your energy.
- o **Rule 13.** Do the bigger tasks first.
- o **Rule 14.** Go with your learning style.
- o **Rule 15.** Avoid procrastination.

Reasons for procrastination:

- o You don't know what you want.
- o You don't have anything to drive you.
- o You're settling.
  - ▪ Stretch yourself.
- o You're overwhelmed.
  - ▪ Begin your game plan.
  - ▪ Take a break.

- o You made it a part of your identity.
    - It's all about how you see yourself.
- o You're a people pleaser.
- o You're dealing with depression.
- o You have low self-esteem.
- o You're just lazy.
    - Push through the laziness.

CHAPTER 13

Counting the Cost

vvvvvvvvvvvvvvvvvvvvvvvvvvvvvvvvvvvvvvvvvvvvvvvvvvvvvvvvvvvvvvvvvvvvvvvvvvv

In This Chapter, I Will Help You:

➤ Understand that sacrifice is a part of the process.

➤ Understand upfront the price tag for your goals.

vvvvvvvvvvvvvvvvvvvvvvvvvvvvvvvvvvvvvvvvvvvvvvvvvvvvvvvvvvvvvvvvvvvvvvvvvvv

Another way to stay consistent is to know upfront the price you'll have to pay to accomplish your goals and prepare yourself for it. Understanding that sacrifice is part of the equation. If you want to lose weight, you have to sacrifice the donuts. If you want to be financially independent, you'll need to sacrifice not giving into those credit cards that keep coming in the mail. If you want to have a better relationship, you must sacrifice your own selfish desires and humble yourself. When you want a baby, you have to sacrifice nine months of your body changing, getting ready to birth that baby out. You see sacrifice to get good results everywhere in life. Sacrifice is also talked about all throughout the Bible. This is the way the world works.

My Sacrifice

As a girl who didn't have a father growing up, I always looked for love in the wrong places. I was in relationships since I was young.

For me personally, I couldn't focus on healing from past pains, finding out who I was, or focus on goals because I was so focused on the relationships.

Around the time I got my first apartment, my bishop in church talked to me about being single for a year, where I can focus on me and growing in God. He was just talking, but I took that as something God was trying to tell me at the time, and I ran with it.

I will tell you, it was one of the hardest things I had to do, especially because I had freedom. I had my ex calling me and people coming out of the woodwork. I was the only single one in my family, and I had my aunties and uncles asking me at weddings when mine was coming. I literally cried some days because it was so hard, but boy, was that sacrifice worth it.

I sacrificed time I wanted to spend on guys for time to invest in me and God. I grew leaps and bounds. That was the year I learned how to hear God's voice so clearly, something I would have had to learn to maintain my marriage now. This was also the year when things broke off me. When I had finally rebuilt the wall of self-confidence.

It was like God was able to get my attention and work on me so I could grow and become a whole person and attract that whole person into my life. Everything that I truly needed to be ready to be Mrs. Right. I had no clue that I was being prepared at the time. Ironically, after the year was complete, I met my husband in 2010.

Meeting My Husband

We had seen each other in church for almost a decade, but never crossed each other's paths. My bishop's wife asked me to get all the young adults together for an event. I always loved to organize, so I always helped in that area.

At that time, Chris wasn't my husband. He went to another church. I went on Facebook and invited a large group to the event through messenger. He was the last person I had added in the group. When I hit send, it said too many people were added, and it wouldn't send. So, I removed him and sent him a single message. To him, he thought I was personally sending him an invite. That was the start of our connection. Through a lot of different occasions, we grew closer and eventually got married. You can meet your significant other in ways you wouldn't have planned.

His Impact on My Life

Meeting the right person changes everything. I wouldn't be the person I am today without my husband. He has helped me in so many ways. Spiritually, he knows that God is the glue that keeps us together, so he would always make sure we pray at night together, and we would talk about the Word of God and how it applies to our life. He helped me grow stronger in God.

I used to be a sensitive person and although I still had traces of that in me, he helped me to understand life more. When I would call him crying because of what a friend did to me, he walked me through it, and I became stronger.

He plays a huge part in me succeeding in my career. Before I became a project manager, I didn't think I had it in me. I didn't think I could even walk into the engineering world; it was so foreign to me. He reminded me that I did have what it takes, and he helped guide me to where I am today. He plays a part in everything in my life. He has helped pave the way for many of my accomplishments. Even this book, he created the book cover, took the pictures, worked on my website, and so much more. He has loved me unconditionally. Our gifts work together well. When we mentor young adults, the combination of our experience, giftings, and personality make an impact on who we talk to. Through every storm that can be thrown at us, (and we have had a lot) we've grown stronger together as each year passes. I'm so glad I took the time to become whole so I could meet a whole person, and we could fulfill our purpose together. I love him with everything in me!

I have everything I ever wanted but had to give up everything I ever had to get it.

The Price Tag

Anytime you want to do anything great in life, it will take hard work. Forget trying to take the easy route with no sacrifices. Those can only get you so far. Every goal has strings attached. There must be some price you pay, which can often be a major roadblock for you. It could be too high, too costly, or not worth what you must give up. You must evaluate the price and let go of the excuses. Let's take a look at different price tags.

Evaluate Your Price Tag

1. **Price Tag 1: Your Time** – Time is your most valuable asset. You definitely want to spend your time wisely. Time isn't something you can get back or pause, but it's something to value and invest in.

   Rachel decides to invest two years of her time studying to become a nurse. At first glance, it seems like this amount of time is forever, but when she looks at her two-year-old son, she realizes that the time flies by, so she might as well invest in it now.

   Tip. Find Options – You can get creative. Find options. When I was studying for my master's degree and working, my time was limited. I found a college with a program that worked with my hours. I would go to school once a week at night for about four hours, and it was across the street from my job. That means, right after work on that day during the week, I would go to school. It was fast track, but it worked great for my schedule. This gave me time to study hard the rest of the week and enjoy time with my loved ones on the weekend.

2. **Price Tag 2: Your Moolah** – It can be a great cost putting money towards your goal. I wish I could say it's free. You have to look at the cost as an investment into your future, and there will be a return for what you've paid.

    Rachel is uneasy about spending a large tuition amount on becoming a nurse. That's money she could be using for other stuff, and money is tight for her right now. After going back and forth in her mind, she realizes that the money she spends now will be an investment that will bring return for her later. She will end up making so much more in just two years than she would if she didn't do anything. The benefit outweighs the cost.

    Getting my MBA cost me loans. I had scholarships, but there was some cost involved. I'm glad I didn't let that stop me because now I'm able to pay it back instead of waiting forever. Not everyone advocates for that, so do what works for you. Just know that sometimes it will require a big chunk of your money.

3. **Price Tag 3: Your Energy** – If you work hard and have a lot of responsibilities, this could be a tough one. You only have so much to give, right? You may be working all day and then come home at night tired and exhausted, but that time window is the only time to get things done. So, instead of using that energy to relax, get extra sleep, and have some fun, you put it towards your goals. I'm doing that as I speak. I got off work, and I didn't feel like doing

squat diddly do, but I pushed myself to put my energy towards my goals.

Rachel has to work a full-time job and go to school. She knows she will be tired when she gets off work. She knows that going to school for nursing is going to take her energy, but she also knows that anything great in life is going to take some sacrifice, and her future self will thank her.

4. **Price Tag 4: Time with Your Loved Ones** – This can really mess with your mind and emotions. If you're a mom of a little one, mommy guilt can creep in big time. It definitely did for me when I had to go back to work. I reminded myself that I had big plans for me and my family. I knew if I prayed about it, I would have some peace, and I'm so glad I did that. It didn't feel good, but it paid off later. I can now afford to enroll my son into a private school and give him the best.

Going to nursing school for Rachel is going to take some time with her child away from her. This brings mommy guilt for Rachel. She had to tell herself that this was also investing in her child's future, and she would work around her schedule to make sure she still had time with her son.

☀️**Tip 1: Get Creative** – You don't have to sacrifice all your time away from your family. You can learn to be creative and manage your time. The problem is people think what they're doing is okay by sacrificing all the time away from their families. Time goes by, and they look up. They've mastered their goals, are doing great financially, but they've lost their families, time they cannot get back.

As someone who is very goal oriented, I had to learn to be creative and make sure I made time for family. When I was in college, I remember my aunt telling me, *"Jennifer, you'll always have goals. You'll finish one, then have another, but make sure you make time for family."*

When I look at her life, she has a demanding career as a nurse. She has a husband and two older girls. She helps a lot of family and friends in the Philippines, and she's an organizer of events, and so much more.

She knows exactly what it's like to be busy, but she always makes it a top priority to spend time with family. She gets to enjoy life to the fullest because she has invested time with her loved ones, created memories, and laughter.

She travels all over the world, and I know she won't have any regrets later in her life because of the time she spent with her family. That's what I desire to be. I took her advice and made a rule: no matter how busy I get, I would make time for my loved ones.

Tip 2: Understand Balance – On the other end of the spectrum, sometimes you invest so much of your time giving to your loved ones, but you invest no time for yourself. You're left unhappy, drained, and not doing anything to take care of yourself. You aren't working out, having any me time for your sanity. You think it's healthy when you can do more by taking care of yourself first, by investing the seed in you. It's important to understand balance.

Shelly is always doing everything for everyone but herself. Everyone calls on her for help, and she says yes without a second thought. She does all the chores at home, she takes the kids to sports. If someone needs a ride or something, she doesn't say no. She runs all the errands and doesn't even think to ask for help. While this is a great trait to have, Shelly is suffering. She doesn't have time for herself. She smiles on the outside, but she's drowning on the inside. Shelly needs to learn balance and setting boundaries.

Whatever excuse you have, someone with your situation or worse is killing it, and they're far surpassing you. They know that in life, it takes work to get what you want.

Let's Tie It All Together

You're almost there! Once you have all these parts under your belt, you can tackle whatever comes your way. You know how to be consistent now by handling distractions and following the rules of the game. Let's take a look at how you can juggle all areas of your life.

Lessons

Another way to stay consistent is to know upfront the price you'll have to pay to accomplish your goals and be prepared for it. Understand that sacrifice is part of the equation.

Evaluate your price tag

- o **Price Tag 1** – Your time
  - ➢ Find options
- o **Price Tag 2** – Your moolah
- o **Price Tag 3** – Your energy
- o **Price Tag 4** – Time with your loved ones
  - ➢ Get creative
  - ➢ Understand balance

PART 6

Balancing it all together

In Part 6...

You've earned everything you need to succeed. Now, let's make sure you can successfully balance it all. Sometimes we can get so focused on one thing, and we master it well, but we forget other areas, and they fail miserably.

In Part 6, we'll look at different domains in your life. These are like categories and will be your spiritual life, family life, health and fitness, finance, career and business, social life, schedule, and focus.

CHAPTER 14

Improving Every Area of Your life

In This Chapter, I Will Provide You With:

➤ Guidelines to improve every area of your life.

➤ Documents to create to help you in balancing your priorities.

Every person is different, so take these as guidelines and concepts, and consider what works best for your life. The purpose is to make sure you have all the puzzle pieces you might not have known you needed. Let's begin.

 1 Improve Your Spiritual Life

In this domain, we'll discuss having a personal relationship with God in your daily life and how to improve your spiritual life. I've also added a section of tips to help your mental and emotional side if you're not a spiritual person.

To have a personal relationship with God, first you must learn to be intimate with Him and talk to Him throughout the day. When I wasn't putting Him first, I was cranky, stressed, and moody, but when I was spending time with Him, things changed.

➤ **Make time for God** – You can also have focus time with Him just like when you have date nights and times when you go out with your friends. When you focus your time on Him, you can find a place where you can be alone with Him. I go to my prayer closet.

You can wake up early in the morning before you start your day, do this late at night, during your lunch, during your commute, or whichever time works best for you. This can be fifteen minutes, thirty minutes, an hour. Just make it a priority to spend time with Him and know the longer you spend with Him, the more you'll grow.

➤ **Your prayer life** – Then, you can spend time in praise and worship, whether you're singing without music or with your favorite praise and worship songs. Always come into prayer with thanksgiving and mean it from your heart. Repent of anything you can think of and forgive those you need to forgive. Then, intercede and pray. Be real with God. Talk to Him from your heart. You can have a list of people you pray for daily, like your family.

The Power of Prayer

You can also have a special request list for those who have requested prayer. Prayer is powerful, and it works. I've experienced my mother healing from aggressive cancer without chemo and my stepdad living through chemo through the power of prayer. I've prayed when I couldn't pay the bills and things were about to get ugly and how at the nick of time, a phone call would happen to take care of my exact situation.

I've had several experiences where I woke up in the middle of the night because I had a specific dream about someone and what they were going through, and God would wake me up to pray for them.

I had a dream of one of the girls I mentor, and she was in danger. I didn't know she was in a serious car accident on life support and was unconscious. A drunk driver had hit her, and her car spiraled out of control onto the highway and ran straight into the median strip. I prayed for her. She said that God spoke to her and told her it wasn't her time. Right then, she woke up from being unconscious for almost a week. She could have died!

One time, I was too lazy to pray. I woke up in the morning of 2017 from a specific dream that I was in a car accident. I didn't think twice about the dream. On my way to work, I got in the worst car accident I've ever been in. I still feel the pain from it.

I've prayed to find my long-lost brother that I couldn't find for years and shortly after that prayer, out of nowhere, I ran into him. I could go on for days about the power of prayer and what it has done in my life.

God is constantly telling you to pray. He also says, in James 4:2b in the Bible, "you have not because you ask not." Come to prayer in faith and do not doubt him. Sometimes you'll come to prayer in a different way than I just explained, and that's okay. Sometimes you may only have a word, or you just want to be silent.

The Struggle

For those who have struggled in prayer and felt like they couldn't feel anything, one thing that has helped me is I close my eyes and focus on all the good things God has done for me. I visualize it in my mind. This does something inside me.

Also, there are times I've been angry and when I go to pray, I don't know what to say. I'm just upset. You can tell Him what's on your mind or you just ask Him for help, or maybe just listen to some praise and worship music or something inspiring to calm your soul. Let the Lord lead you and make sure your focus is on having an authentic relationship with Him.

➢ **Read Your Bible** – The Bible is your guidance to live. Sometimes it can be hard to read. I love the "Action Bible: God's Redemptive Story," by Doug Mauss. It has helped me understand the Old Testament, maybe because I'm a visual learner. This book is almost like a comic book, filled with imagery. Since I'm a visual learner, I understand reading the Bible stories much better than just staring at words with no images.

I also like, "The Action Bible," by Sergio Cariello that I use with, "What the Bible is all about," by Dr. Henrietta C. Mears, and a notebook to jot notes. It helps me understand the New Testament. For example, the four Gospels (Matthew, Mark, Luke, and John), this book explains the different viewpoints each man told when telling the story about Jesus.

They explain it very well. I never looked at it that way, and it helps me as I read. If there are any other books you would like to read to help you with your spiritual walk, feel free to do that.

➤ **Other ways to get close to God** – It's also good to have a journal where you can talk to God about your thoughts and struggles. The more real you are, the better. I've also created declaration sheets, which is anything I wanted to see in my life.

On these declarations, I would declare that I already have it, and eventually with time, strategy, and work, it came to pass. For example, here are some things I would declare when I was engaged in 2010 that I didn't quite have yet, but I now have in my life.

Declarations

✓ I'm emotionally, mentally, and spiritually strong.

✓ Whatever I put my mind to, I accomplish.

✓ I have a beautiful wedding (and I would go into detail how I wanted my wedding to be).

✓ I have a happy and blessed marriage.

✓ I have a beautiful home I can afford in a nice neighborhood.

✓ I'm in my best health now.

✓ I spread love and joy to all those around me.

✓ I'm living my dream job.

✓ I have an amazing son.

I laminated my sheet to keep from messing it up. You can also take this time to visualize, memorize a weekly scripture, and focus your mind on the good things God has done for you and where he's going to take you.

➤ **Find a church home/community** – It's good to be under a covering, a church that can help you grow and feed you. I've been in a season where I wasn't connected for a few years. I could definitely tell the difference. It's like I was sinking alone. I didn't have the support I needed, nor was I growing. It was when I was connected that made the difference.

Spiritual Parents / Spiritual Mentors

There will be divine appointments, people who will give you your spiritual inheritance. Find your spiritual parents or spiritual mentors, become involved, and grow. I know that some people have been hurt by church but understand that people aren't perfect. Just because there was one bad apple, doesn't mean they're all the same. Don't let them miss out on your growth. Remember, the key is having a relationship with God.

I've grown tremendously and have met key milestones in my life by having my spiritual parents and spiritual mentors in my life. When I was about fifteen years old, I went to this youth group and became close to Pastor CJ. Over the next five years, he would impart so much spiritual wisdom into my life that would carry me throughout my adult years.

This was the time I came out of my shell, because I was extremely shy. Pastor CJ saw something inside me that I didn't know I had. He wanted me to become a Testifier for Christ. That means I would go on stage every week in front of a hundred inner-city teenagers and encourage them in life and testify about God's goodness. I developed during that time and found my voice. I met amazing people. There are people who see your potential before you do and help bring out the best in you.

It also helped me during some of the darkest times in my life because I was plugged into something good. One of those struggles was living with a crazy stepfather who ended up going to jail. The police were over our house all the time. At one point, my mom had a restraining order. One time, I was about to get in my car, and the neighbor said, "Hey, I don't mean to be nosy, but is he supposed to be at the house?"

I quickly said, "No, if you see him, call the cops."

My mom and I had some unexpected event we had to go to. Later on, when we got back home, my neighbor told me she saw him sneak into the backyard, and they called the cops. The cops found him hiding in the attic. Luckily, no one was in the house.

I had a lot of anger towards this man. It was a difficult season for me. The lessons Pastor CJ imparted in me and the people I was surrounded with kept me strong during these times. It made a world of difference. The support system can help you through the darkest times.

As I got older, there were many other spiritual mentors in my life from Mr. Mark, Pastor Mike, Lashawn, Shana, and more. Mr. Mark tried to help me understand the world around me and to realize how special I was.

Pastor Mike tried to help me stop making huge mistakes with guys. He gave an analogy like I was in a valuable car but kept crashing it. Lashawn told me her story when she was in a relationship. She gave me the unfiltered story, but through her mistakes, she pushed in God, and I saw her life blossom. Her story always encouraged me and helped me to fight. Shana told me whatever I do, don't settle. Her words always rang in my ears when I wanted them.

Before I met my husband, I went to a church and met my spiritual parents. A lot of wisdom and mentoring was imparted in my life through them. They helped me to heal from a lot of pain from my past, navigated me through the storms in my life, and prepared me to meet my husband. That's where I met him by the way, in that same church.

Before I ever had spiritual leadership in my life, I always prayed for guidance that I didn't have since my father had passed away. These people were an answered prayer, and I wouldn't be who I am today without all them coming across my path.

You can pray for God to bring these people in your life and seek these places until you find peace. You'll feel good when you're in a place that will help you grow, and there are people around you who love you and will pray for you.

Large Churches / Small Churches

Within large churches, sometimes you can feel lost and disconnected. Find out if they have small groups that fit you. In small churches, you can become more involved and do what you're most able to do. These people will be your family. In the Bible, Ecclesiastes 4:10 says, "Two are better than one, because they have a good return for their labor. For if one falls down, his companion can lift him up; but pity the one who falls without another to help him up." When one falls, and no one is there to help them whole, but if two are together, it's good, and it's like a triple-braided cord.

> ➢ **Be a blessing to others** – You can also find ways to give back with your time, money, and/or talent. It's like thanking God. You can volunteer in your church, get involved in the community, create programs to help others, create ministries, or just do caring things for your loved ones.

> ➢ **If you're not a spiritual person** – Maybe you're not a spiritual person. If this applies to you, one thing you can focus on is the inner you. You want to be emotionally, mentally, and spiritually strong. A couple of my close friends have said meditation ten to fifteen minutes a day helps out tremendously. It brings a sense of peace to the chaos.

> You can also work on finding self-help books to help you improve on certain weak areas of your life. For example, maybe you have an anger problem. There are books out there talking about how to overcome that. Lastly, you can find a

group that you can connect to, to keep you encouraged. Find ways to help your inner man be emotionally and mentally strong.

 ## 2 Improve Your Relationships

Family to you can mean something completely different to someone else. Some people are single and are animal lovers. It's just them and their cat or dog. Others are married or have kids. Find what concepts you can take with you. Sometimes we get so busy, our family time suffers. It's important to make time for your family and create rituals.

➤ **Create rituals** – Rituals can be date nights with your significant other, time with your kids—whoever is considered your loved one. Find a consistent time you spend with them. Maybe it's once a week, once a month, maybe it's just giving them a call to check on them. Just don't forget this area. While you're at it, make time for yourself too, called "*me*" time. You can pamper yourself through getting massages, getting your nails done, resting, doing something for yourself, especially when you're usually the one doing everything for everyone else. You can also go shopping. It's important to treat yourself. If you don't take care of your own needs, you can't give the best to your family.

➤ **Make time to travel** – It's always good to travel. Make plans for a vacation. You can do it once a year, once a quarter, whatever you can afford. Live life to the fullest! Get a budget, a date, an agenda, and action items.

Inspired by my aunt, who always went on vacations around the world with her family, creating memories and taking pictures, I finally planned for vacations. The first month, we went to Branson, MO, just a few hours away from where we live. It was an amazing time. The second time, we went to Miami, FL and went on the beach. We don't have beaches in Oklahoma. That experience was so amazing, especially experiencing the difficult cultures when it came to the people and the food. Another place we went to was Disney World. It was so much fun.

If the planning seems overwhelming, I recommend a travel agent. Disney World is huge, and I didn't have all the time to plan every detail; it was a bit overwhelming. I got a travel agent to help guide me through the process. It was great!

➢ **Invest in Your Relationships** – Another goal is finding ways to invest in your relationships. This could be getting together and helping each other become stronger.

For my husband and I, we've listened to podcasts, watched videos, and read books that talk about marriage, finances, our personalities, etc. You can do anything that brings your relationship together to make you all stronger, like learning more about each other and how to resolve issues.

Weekly Marriage Meetings

Since my husband and I are organized and business minded, we've found that having meetings once a week to invest in our relationship and goals has been successful. We call these meetings CJ Meetings. The C stands for Chris, and J stands for Jennifer, our names. We've been doing this for over a decade, even before we were married, and it has been beneficial.

It has helped us work together through buying a home, preparing for a child, organizing large trips, and organizing our business launches together. It has also helped us in tackling financial roadblocks, finding out what can be improved in our responsibilities at home, getting our son enrolled into another school, talking about big decisions in our life, new budgets, and the list goes on.

We would talk it through together and have action items to work on and follow up the next week. I remember telling my sister about these meetings, and she said she can just talk to her significant other; she didn't need a meeting for that.

That's good, but sometimes there are a lot of things that need to get done, and tasks can fall through the cracks if you don't write it down. When she went for pre-marital counseling, the pastor also mentioned the importance of having these meetings and how it has blessed his marriage. He has been married for a long time. I didn't talk to him about this; he just knew about it and the benefits. She started doing it, enjoyed it, and found it helpful. This is now part of her marriage.

When you do have these meetings, function in your strength, and let the other person do that as well. For example, I'm the one who puts the documents together, adds the action items, and is more of the execution type. My husband is more the logical type. He's good at making sure what I do is done correctly. A lot of the time, we need to come up with more research or a better strategy. I'm glad he does this because it avoids problems down the line. I'm good at making sure what's assigned gets done. Practice and find what suits your relationship.

There are times our personalities can clash. I like to know things way ahead of time, and my husband likes to know it when it's closer. Sometimes that causes us to butt heads. This can happen when I want to plan a vacation further out.

One time, I was eager to plan for a house. I had all my research done. When we were in the meeting, he didn't feel it was the time. I was so upset. After some clashes of our personalities, we found a good balance. We would meet each other halfway.

It's important to be balanced in this meeting. It's also important not to make the other person feel bad, where it forfeits the purpose of the meeting. For example, sometimes my husband doesn't get some action items done. I don't get all upset or make him feel bad. He'll tell me what happened and will assign a new date.

While I do keep him accountable, I won't roll my eyes, sigh, or make him feel like these meetings are a waste of time. Even though my personality can be triggered to do that. We find ways to tweak what isn't working. Now, if he keeps dropping the ball every week, then I can be a little bit firmer, just like anyone would be when holding someone accountable.

If you don't have much to talk about or don't want to be formal, then feel free to have a discussion without a meeting. The meetings just help you stay on track, help things not fall through the cracks, and propel your marriage forward as you work together as a team. If you're interested in having a meeting, I have listed a format below on how we run our meetings.

The Meeting Format

✓ **Last week's action items** – Right after I say a quick prayer for God to lead us and guide us in our decisions, I talk about our action items from last week. This is on the top of the document. I like to discuss this first in the meeting right after I pray. I just carry over the action items from last week's meeting and see if we can check them off or roll them over to next week. If it got done, I check it off. If it didn't, we talk about it, and I add it into current action items I talk about below.

✓ **Agenda** – After we discuss last week's action items, we go over the agenda. Sometimes if we just talked about it, I just skip that topic. For the agenda, this can be ongoing topics or ones we decided to add. Sometimes during the week, I think of stuff I want to talk about, and I just add it to this document. Examples can be finances, big ticket items, vacations, discussion on big decisions, how to improve habits, ways to invest in the marriage, etc. I always ask him if there's anything else I need to add.

✓ **Action items** – As we're talking, new action items might come up, so I list this in this section. I always put who is going to be over the action items, sometimes it's both of us. I also have a date we want to finish it. Sometimes I'm general, and I'll say this week.

This whole process can take anywhere from ten minutes to one hour, depending on how much you have to talk about. On average, it takes us about thirty minutes once a week.

After I'm done, I save the file with the date we did the meeting and send him a copy, so he knows what to work on. Then we finish by reading a book we choose together that invests in our marriage. We only read a small section, that takes about five to ten minutes.

The books we've read have taught us the difference between men and women. I understood a lot about why men go into their caves or how they handle stress, and he understood why women need to talk and how we handle stress. We learned how to speak our love languages and how to handle conflict. These books have been great.

Good Books We Read

✓ *"The Seven Principles for Making Marriage Work"* – by John Gottman

✓ *"Love & Respect"* – by Dr. Emerson Eggerichs

✓ *"Men Are from Mars and Women Are from Venus" –* by John Gray

➢ **Responsibilities** – Other areas to improve in your relationship are your responsibilities. What chores do you have? Are you doing it by yourself? Together? What works best for you and your family? Sometimes that's doing fifteen to thirty minutes a day, other times it's doing it one big day during your time off. I find that tidying the house throughout the week and doing a deep clean on my days off works best for me.

For laundry, I try to wash all the clothes on the weekend and fold it, but I always end up doing a load a day and then folding the clothes on the weekend. There are different ways to do this.

 ## 3 Improve Your Health

Health is everything. You can be knocking out your goals left and right, but if your life is short-lived, you only hurt yourself. My father had his own business, had houses, and a lot of family, but he had poor health. The result from poor health was that he passed away at the age of forty-four years old.

I used to always get sick. I had acid reflux, pain in my hips, and I've passed out five to ten times in my life. I've passed out at work, on airplanes, in people's homes, in restaurants, you name it. I've felt a lot of pain on the inside of my body and had constant headaches. When it came to weight, I had gained fifty pounds after having a child.

I went through everything to try to lose weight. I did Weight Watchers, Atkins, Herbal Life, the Dukan Diet, the Grapefruit Juice Diet, the Lemonade diet, Keto, taken pills, and more. Sometimes I would lose weight, but I felt horrible during the process, or it wasn't sustainable. I could look at a donut and gain all that weight back. Everything changed when I found a nutrition regimen that worked for me.

➢ **Find the nutrition regimen that works for you** – I finally mastered my nutrition, and it wasn't without help from my close friend Lucretia. She introduced me to the plant-based world. In the very beginning, before I was convinced, I remember laughing at her more than once when she thought I would give up meat. I'm a meat lover, are you kidding me?

She coached me through the new lifestyle. I tried it out, and I immediately felt all the pain go away in my body. Previously, we would also work out to videos, and I would run out of breath and need water. After going plant based, all that stopped. This new way of eating was very doable for me. I lost a lot of body fat and have kept it off for quite some time. I'm full of energy, I get full easily, and all in all feel great.

The food wasn't bad. I just found what worked for me. It actually tasted good. I'm not much of a cook, but stir fry vegetables with rice, curry, big salads with beans, veggie burritos, they all tasted great.

I also became a lover of green smoothies. I followed JJ Smith's book the "10-Day Green Smoothie Cleanse." This will jumpstart your weight loss and cleanse all the junk out of you. The weight dropped off me, the smoothies kept me full, and they tasted great. They are easy to make. Once you have all the ingredients, it takes one minute to make. I just got myself a blender and bought the frozen fruit and everything she requested. To keep me full, I added Vega protein powder.

After those ten days, I followed her book, "Green Smoothies for Life." Green smoothies are a way of life for me. I drink them for snacks, and it's a good way to get a lot of vegetables and fruits in me.

When I don't feel like cooking, I go to places I can get vegan food and try to stay away from processed foods, leaning more towards plant-based foods. Since I don't cook on the weekends, I always go to places to get food.

One guy makes soul food out of his house. His food is absolutely delicious, and it's all plant based. He makes spaghetti, lasagna, burgers, brisket, and the list goes on. I'm a regular customer. There are so many options out there.

I joined a Facebook group for vegans in my area and have gotten so many suggestions. There's a document that has about one hundred and thirty-four pages of places to go with pictures. Find a community and do your research, prepare, and you'll set yourself up for success,

My husband has come to love plant based with me. In the beginning, he laughed at giving up his meat. After he saw my results and watched, "What the Health," he was sold.

The video talks about what happens to your body when you eat meat and what happens behind the scenes to those who sell it to you. It also talks about the amazing benefits of a plant-based life and how you can still get fit. There are amazing testimonies on there. You can find this video on Netflix. My husband immediately saw weight drop off his body, and his constant headaches disappeared.

I've been consistent all throughout 2020, even through the holidays, and it isn't difficult. Your body will crave only the healthy food it needs. For Thanksgiving, I just brought a big vegan dish, and I could find other vegan foods. I was full. One thing I notice is I can eat a lot of the vegan food and not gain any weight. This was much different from when I was on yo-yo diets; it was easy to gain the weight back.

The closer you get to plant-based foods from the earth, the healthier you'll be. If you have the right nutrition regimen, and you make time for food prep and fitness, not only will you have your dream body, you'll get your energy back and feel amazing. Find what works for your life, whether you're trying to lose weight, maintain, or gain.

➤ **Food prep** – Choose a day to food prep. You can do it once a week, a little throughout the day, or make a big meal, have leftovers, and then start again. Also, choose a day during the week to create your shopping list and a day to pick up your groceries. I like to save time and order my groceries online. I then just have the stores load the groceries into my car. This has saved hours out of my week.

➢ **Fitness** – As a beginner in the fitness world, I started off walking because I loved it. I just committed to thirty minutes a day, five times a week. Once I gained confidence in that area, I went to the next level and added weights. The walking can slim you down, but you don't want a skinny fat body; you want your body to change its shape and be sexy underneath those clothes.

I admit, I did a lot of research and was confused on what to do as a beginner. I decided to find a YouTube video and follow their format. I ended up choosing to do strength training two to three times a week, following the plan I had written down. For me, I focused on the full body. I kept adding weights as I got stronger.

When I first started out, I wanted to throw up and pass out. It was so difficult. After some consistency, my body got stronger, and it became easier, so I continued to stretch myself. The results were amazing; the inches dropped off fast, and I liked what I saw.

I'm now moving to the next level, by being trained and working out with fitness gurus. The point is to start off with what you know and make sure you make time for working out. You can do this first thing in the morning, at lunch, or in the evening. I've done them all. I like doing it first thing in the morning, but sometimes I have other priorities to get done. So, I'm currently doing it during my lunch time, while I work from home.

4 Improve Your Finances

Most people, if not everyone, wants to be financially independent. There are many roads to get there. First, just focus on knowing the basics. You want to have a budget, manage your money well, save, have good credit, and have passive income. You must eventually get to the place where you don't work for money, as it works for you.

Financial Documents to Have

➢ **A budget** – You'll put the amount of money you know based off your spending habits and needs.

  ▪ **Example**

    ✓ Your ten percent tithe.

    ✓ Your expenses.

    ✓ Your cost of living. Cost of living would be food, transportation/gas, house/utilities.

    ✓ A safety net for small miscellaneous.

    ✓ Surplus. Whatever money you have left is your surplus. Not everyone has a surplus. If you do, you want to use it for savings, investments, off books, or goals you want to reach like paying down your debt.

➢ **A payment list** – This has all your bills and the due dates in order. I have a document that lists every bill, when it's due, and any information I may need to know like the link to pay it online. I like to pay my bills one week ahead of time, every weekend. Every time I pay the bill, I mark an X to show I paid it. This helps me keep track.

Example of a Payment List

SAMPLE	Cost	Due Date	Automatic	JANUARY PAID	WEBSITE / INFORMATION
RENT	$ 700.00	1st		X	
ELECTRIC	$ 100.00	5th		X	OGE.COM
CELL PHONE BILL	$ 150.00	20th	A		TMOBILE.COM

➢ **Checks and balances** – Also, keep track of where your money goes and when you pay things. I create a checks and balances sheet to do this. I look at this weekly. The point is to make sure the numbers match.

For example, my bank account will show I have five hundred and fifty dollars in my account. On my list, it'll show me what all the money I have is assigned too.

✓ Tithe $55
✓ Internet $50
✓ Savings $350
✓ Off Books (spending money) $95
Total: $550

Every week, I look at my bank account and if something has gone through, I remove it from this document. When I pay bills, I make a note in this document the day I paid it. That way I don't think I have more money than I thought.

More Financial Areas Of improvement

> **Savings** – Your savings can be for an emergency fund on a rainy day. You can have one thousand dollars, three to six months of expenses saved, or more. You can have savings for house maintenance, car maintenance, vacations, and if you have children, their college, and any big-ticket items you want.

> **Investments** – You can have money going towards growing your investments in stocks, crypto, investing in real estate, or your own business.

> **Becoming debt free** – You can have a plan to become debt free if you've accumulated any debt or feel it has gotten out of control. You can do this many ways, by using the snowball effect that Dave Ramsey talks about in his book, "The Total Money Makeover." The snowball effect means you start off with paying the smallest debt first. After that's paid, you go on to the next smallest bill. You keep going until all the debt has been paid off.

Another way is to start off with paying the high-interest debt. You can also get into programs that consolidate your debt into one big payment, sometimes saving you more money or debt resolution programs. They'll save you money, but it may temporarily hurt your credit score until everything is resolved.

➢ **Improve your credit score** – If your credit score is suffering and you want to improve it, you'll want to come up with a plan. Good credit can open many good doors for you. Some people don't care about this since they want to pay everything in cash. Again, do what works for you.

First, you need to understand why your credit score is bad. You can use Credit Karma to assess your debt. Some people have poor credit because they don't have any credit. You can get a secure card to build your credit score. That means you put money on the card and keep paying it. My husband started off with more credit because he didn't have any credit history. He got some secure credit cards and built his credit. His credit increased significantly.

Maybe you have too many credit cards, and you've used up most of your utilization. That means you almost or already have maxed out your credit cards and only pay the minimum payment. You can improve your credit score significantly by getting a personal loan and paying off those credit cards through consolidation. Your utilization will go down.

There are many programs out there to help you. I have been in this situation before and when I got a personal loan to pay off my credit cards, my credit score increased forty points in one month.

➢ **Passive income** – Another thing you want to look at is finding ways to build passive income by doing the things you love. There are so many ways to do this. Find your gift, and a way to do this. Is there a service or product you can provide? What about knowledge you can give out through writing, speaking, coaching, or consulting?

➢ **Growing your income** – If you're working, find a way to grow your income. Get an education, build your skill, and if you aren't happy with the money where you work, find a higher-paying job and be ready for it. Don't tell the next place how much you made. Tell them what you can give and look at the market industry rate, and that will be what you want and should expect. If they low ball you, negotiate or keep on going.

5 Improve Your Career & Business

It's always good to invest in your dreams, whether that's a career job or starting your own business. You can take aptitude tests to determine what you want to do. Research what schools you want to attend, the application process, and the tuition costs.

➢ **Earning your career** – You can invest in yourself now and get grants and loans through your FAFSA and pay it back afterwards, or you can pay it out of cash or get a lot of scholarships. See what support the schools provide and fill them out.

Once you narrow down the college, talk to an advisor to help you apply, fill out your FAFSA, and get your books. Before you know it, you'll be enrolled, you'll have your study plan, and time will fly by, and you'll be walking across the stage.

I highly recommend getting your education. Don't make excuses. People busier than you are doing it. People older than you are doing it, so you can make it happen. Once you have your education, find a job you love. Please don't settle or let any of the companies limit you. Find one that you love and do your best at it.

My cousin Tina has three children: ages one, two, and nine years old. Tina wanted to do more in her life, but she was scared to go to school. She wasn't sure she had what it took. She knew she would have to take basic classes like math, and that scared her. She also was a mother of three. How would she find the time? I encouraged Tina. "If your heart is in it, go for it. Timing is moving anyways, and it's moving fast. You might as well do it. You'll look up and be walking across the stage."

Tina is happy she went ahead and pursued her career in social work. She wasn't sure what to do at first, but she realized taking it one step at a time, researching, and asking questions would get her where she needs to go. She just had to start. Years have already flown by, and she's almost done with her education. She's setting herself up for success for herself and her family because she decided to take the step to getting her education.

➤ **Starting your own business** – If you want to start your own business, research everything it will take to get started. Have an idea of what product or service you want to provide, then create a business plan, which will consist of you talking about your product or service, your target market, how you'll market your business, the operations, the finances, etc.

Make sure you have a plan. Please don't just come up with an idea and jump into it, as you're only setting yourself up for stress and failure. Do it the right way. Do it just like successful organizations do it. When you're ready, get your business name official, get your brand created, and all the bells and whistles to make it happen.

6 Improve Your Personal Life

Personal goals make you better—it could be hobbies or anything personal for you. I use this domain for fun projects I'm working on, just for the fun of it. For example, remodeling my house, redoing my wardrobe, creating another vision boards, etc.

I also use personal goals for reading. The most successful people read a lot of books. You can start off with thirty minutes a day and work your way up. Find books you enjoy; find books on topics you want to learn.

You can listen to audio books if you're not much of a reader or if you're a busy person. The best times for me to listen to audio books is when I'm getting ready for work, commuting to work and home, or cleaning up the house. I would finish the book in a week or two.

Since I'm a consistent reader, and I get through the books quickly, I use a service called Audible on my phone. I pay fifteen dollars a month which turns into a credit. Once I am ready to purchase another book, I use that credit.

There are some audio books out there that can cost almost twenty dollars, but if you sign up at audible.com, you end up only paying fifteen dollars for one book. Another nice thing is, if you get busy for a couple months or so, you end up having credits saved up, and you can use them all.

7 Improve Your Social Life

The social domains are to make sure you invest in your relationships. These are close friends and family, people other than your immediate family. You want to be around those who help sharpen you. Put effort into setting time to meet them face to face. If you can't meet them, call them, check on them in text, or do a video call. You never know what people are going through. Remember relationships are what make the journey worthwhile.

My sister and I have sister dates once a month, and we love them. We love catching up on life and encouraging each other. One of my best friends lives in Indianapolis. Almost ten hours from me when you drive. We met in college and distance didn't separate us. We almost talked every day for over ten years. My husband was amazed at how consistent we were. We've done this through the busyness of working, getting married, having kids, and starting our own business. We've had the best talks.

Another one of my friends lives in Japan. When it's my morning time, it's her nighttime, yet we talk all the time using an application called Marco Polo. I'll leave her a video and when she gets to it, she'll listen to it and respond. We've left videos while we were laughing hard, crying, frustrated, angry, or excited sharing our journey.

I'm also working on having breakfast with my mom every other week. I do this with other family and friends. Sometimes I may just text them. The point is to make time for the ones you love. Those relationships count.

8 Improve Your Schedule

Your schedule domain is just your current schedule. It's important because it's what you do on a daily basis. I like to use this as a domain so I can reflect on what's working and what's not.

9 Improve What You Focus On

Lastly, you have your focus domain. What will your concentration be on this season? I like to have this one here because

I want to always have this on the forefront of my mind. Review these on a daily or weekly basis to make sure you're growing in every area.

You now have everything you need to succeed...

You now have everything you need to succeed. Beat the inner you, and remove all barriers that might stop you in your tracks. Discover your vision and create goals that bring you towards it. Break down those goals into tasks and prioritize and estimate how long it will take. Know the difference between projects and habits.

Know your current schedule and create your future schedule. Once you're done with that, implement your future schedule into your current schedule. Your blueprint is now created. Get all your tools in place, stay organized, follow the steps to being consistent, and make sure every area of your life is thriving. Know that you can and will always succeed. Nothing can ever stop you. You were made to win!

Lessons

Improve your spiritual life

- o Focus time with God.
- o Your prayer life.
- o Read your Bible.
- o Other ways to get close to God.
- o Find a church home/community.
- o Be a blessing to others.

Improve your relationships

- o Create rituals.
- o Make time to Travel.
- o Invest in your relationships.
  - ➢ Weekly marriage meetings
- o Responsibilities.

Improve your health

- o Choose the right nutrition regimen.
- o Food prep.
- o Fitness.

Improve your finances

- o Financial Documents to Have
  - ➢ A budget
  - ➢ A payment list
  - ➢ Savings
  - ➢ Investments
  - ➢ Improve Your Credit Score

- ➢ Passive Income
- ➢ Growing Your Income

Improve your career and business

- o Getting Your Career
- o Starting Your Own Business

Improve your personal life

Improve your schedule

Improve what you focus on

Please share your progress with me!

I'm so happy that you came across my book. I know you can do it!
You have everything it takes! I would love to hear your progress,
and if you need any help along the way, you can contact me at
organizethreesixty.com.
Go and make your dreams come true and create a legacy!

47698984R00125